P9-EDS-256

BADMINTON

GOODYEAR
Physical Activities Series

Edited by J. Tillman Hall

Archery	Jean A. Barrett *California State University, Fullerton*
Badminton	James Poole *California State University, Northridge*
Bowling	Norman E. Showers *Southern Illinois University*
Fencing	Nancy L. Curry *Southwest Missouri State College*
Folk Dance	J. Tillman Hall *University of Southern California*
Golf	Edward F. Chui *University of Hawaii*
Handball	Pete Tyson *University of Texas*
Men's Basketball	Richard H. Perry *University of Southern California*
Men's Gymnastics	Gordon Maddux *California State University, Los Angeles*
Paddleball and Racquetball	A. William Fleming *Florida International University* Joel A. Bloom *University of Houston*
Soccer	John Callaghan *University of Southern California*
Social Dance	John G. Youmans *Temple University*

Swimming	Donald L. Gambril *Harvard University*
Fundamentals of **Physical Education**	J. Tillman Hall *University of Southern California*
	Kenneth C. Lersten *University of Southern California*
	Merril J. Melnick *University of Southern California*
	Talmage W. Morash *California State University, Northridge*
	Richard H. Perry *University of Southern California*
	Robert A. Pestolesi *California State University, Long Beach*
	Burton Seidler *California State University, Los Angeles*
Volleyball	Randy Sandefur *California State University, Long Beach*
Tennis	Barry C. Pelton *University of Houston*
Women's Basketball	Ann Stutts *California State University, Northridge*
Women's Gymnastics	Mary L. Schreiber *California State University, Los Angeles*

GOODYEAR PUBLISHING COMPANY, INC.
Pacific Palisades, California

Goodyear Physical Activities Series
J. Tillman Hall: *Series Editor*

James Poole
California State University, Northridge

SECOND EDITION
BADMINTON

Acknowledgments

I would like to thank Herbert Scheele of England, who assisted in the area of history and gave permission as secretary of the International Badminton Federation to reprint the laws of badminton. I also deeply thank David Ogata and Ken Purdy for the photography and also all of the American players who allowed their photographs to be used in this book. Finally, my deepest thanks to Dr. George Ziegenfuss and Carl Loveday who gave me inspiration and encouragement in my younger days of competition in badminton and other sports.

Second Edition

Copyright © 1973, 1969 by
GOODYEAR PUBLISHING COMPANY, INC.
Pacific Palisades, California

All rights reserved. No part of this book may be reproduced in any form or by any means without permission in writing from the publisher.

Library of Congress Catalog Card Number: 72-90982

Current printing (last number):
10 9 8 7 6 5 4 3 2 1

ISBN: 0-87620-089-7
Y-0897-2
Printed in the United States of America

Contents

Student/Teacher Instructional Objectives

Editor's note

The Goodyear Publishing Company presents a series of physical education books written by instructors expert in their respective fields.

These books on major sports are intended as supplementary material for the instructor and to aid the student in the understanding and mastery of the sport of his choice. Each book covers its fundamentals—the beginning techniques, rules and customs, equipment and terms—and gives to the reader the spirit of the sport.

Each author of this series brings to the reader the knowledge and skill he has acquired over many years of teaching and coaching. We sincerely hope that these books will prove invaluable to the college student or any student of the sport.

In BADMINTON, James Poole presents the history, terms, equipment, fundamental to advanced skills, and strategy of this popular game. From his experience at Louisiana State University and California State University, Northridge, and as the men's singles champion in the United States, James Poole is able to bring the student a comprehensive analysis of badminton.

This book reveals the early history of badminton and describes its development from the courts of England to the gymnasiums of the United States. The author has included many line drawings and photographs that clearly illustrate all foot, hand, and body positions essential to master this game. He also includes a set of self-testing standards by which the student can evaluate his progress as he acquires the basic techniques. Court specifications, and the rules and their interpretations are also covered. Badminton is a sport that is still growing in popularity; it is quick, challenging, and fun.

The tear out student/teacher evaluation forms included in this revised book should be a real asset to both the teacher and the student.

BADMINTON

History

The origin of badminton is somewhat cloudy; documents show evidence of the game having been played in several countries. A version of badminton in China used wooden paddles and a ball. There is some mention of the game as far back as the twelfth century in the royal court records of England. There is also evidence that a member of the royal family of Poland played it in the late seventeenth or early eighteenth centuries. In India it was played at Poona, and called by that name for some time in the 1870s. It has not been clearly established whether English army officers took the game to India or brought it to England from India. What is definitely known is that the name *badminton* comes from the town of Badminton, home of the Duke of Beaufort.

Mr. H.A.E. Scheele, present Secretary of the International Badminton Federation (IBF), offered the following information about the origin of the game:

> ... I would say that to the best of my knowledge it is quite clear that the game was first played at the home of the Duke of Beaufort which is situated in a town called Badminton in Gloucestershire, which is not very far from Bristol. There is even some uncertainty as to the date of the invention. One or two books written many years ago have

given certain dates of about 1870, but the present Duke told me himself a few years ago that he was quite convinced that the date must have been 3—4 years earlier than that.

Where the first club was is also quite a mystery, and this is not particularly surprising. In the old days of about 100 years ago such things as clubs did not exist for anything as they do now, and the game will have been restricted altogether in early years to being played in the enormous drawing room possessed by the aristocracy. However, I have always understood that Folkestone did form the first club, though I may be biased in being guilty of wishful thinking because Folkstone is in my own county of Kent.

There exists nothing in the way of printed historical information and the earliest book written on the game was not published until 1911. This was a book called *Badminton* by S.M. Massey, a well-known player early in the century and a man of some inportance at the time in the administration, such as it was, of the game.

The original rules of the game were drawn up in 1877, revised in 1887, and again in 1890. The present rules of the IBF differ only slightly from the 1890 draft.

Prior to 1901, when the present court dimensions and shape were adopted, courts varied considerably, although most were of the hourglass shape. This shape can be traced back to the Duke of Beaufort's room in which badminton was played. Two doors opened inwards on the side walls near the net area, and it was decided to narrow the court at the net in order to allow nonplayers to enter and leave the room without disturbing play, hence the hourglass shaped court. As the for size of the court, one at Ealing in West London measured 60' by 30', and it is believed that local players on this court had some advantage over their visitors in matches. It was quite common to play three to four to a side in those days, while singles matches were unknown.

The first All-England championships were held in 1897 and were completed in one day, in contrast to the elaborate arrangements and four days now required to finish the meeting. The success of this first meeting served as a great impetus to the game throughout the British Isles.

The Badminton Union of Ireland was founded in 1889 and promoted its first championship in 1902. The first international match between England and Ireland was played in 1903. The Scottish championships were first played at Aberdeen in 1907, and the union was formed in 1911. *The Badminton Gazette*, which is still the official journal of the Badminton Association of England, was founded in 1907 and is now nearing its fiftieth volume.

These early tournaments did much to encourage the game and were very popular with the players. Players from other countries came to England to play and to learn the game, and teams played matches in Europe. In 1925 and 1930 an English team toured Canada, and influenced the increase of badminton in the United States and Canada. The Canadian Badminton Association was formed in 1931, and the American Badminton Association (ABA) in 1936. The founding of the International Badminton Federation in 1934 helped to foster international play. Sir George Thomas, a famous English player and administrator of the game, presented the Thomas Cup (run on almost identical lines as tennis's Davis Cup) to be challenged for by members of the IBF. After a setback caused by the outbreak of war in 1939, the first International Competition for the Thomas Cup was inaugurated in 1948—49. Ten countries playing in three zones competed in the first competition, which resulted in a win for Malaya, whose team beat Denmark in the finals at Preston, England, in February, 1949. This competition is held every three years.

In 1950, Mrs. H.S. Uber, still considered by many to be the finest lady mixed doubles player the game has ever known, felt it was time that the ladies be included in international competition. She donated the magnificent trophy bearing her name, and the Ladies International Badminton Championship, for Uber Cup competition, was born. The first competition for the cup was played in 1957; subsequent competitions are at three-year intervals. The first competition was won by the United States.

For the most part, the top players in the world come from the Far East. Perhaps the reason is that badminton is considered the national game in Malaysia, Indonesia, and Thailand and a player is treated as we in the United States would treat a football or baseball hero. The tournaments and Thomas Cup competitions in Djakarta and Singapore will play before 10 to 15 thousand spectators.

The first American championships were held in 1937 in Chicago, with Walter Kramer of Detroit winning the men's singles and Mrs. Dell Barkuff of Seattle the ladies' singles. Since then (except for the war years during the forties, when it wasn't played) the United States Nationals has been held in different cities throughout the country. Starting in 1954, the United States Nationals became an "open" championship which allowed foreigners to compete. The open nationals was advocated by many officials in hopes of improving the quality of American Play. In 1970, the United States Nationals went to a "closed" and "open" championships. Only American residents are eligible to play in the closed with selected Americans and all foreign players eligible for the open events.

The United States has never won the Thomas Cup, but has won the Uber Cup on several occasions. Even though we might not be among the best in international play, it is interesting that perhaps the top man and woman players of all time come from the United States. Dr. David G. Freeman maintained an amazing record of not having been defeated in singles play from 1939 until 1953, when he finally retired, beating the best players in the world in 1949 when he met them in Thomas Cup and All-England play. On the distaff side, Judy Devlin Hashman has won over 31 United States national titles and 17 All-England titles since 1954. She officially retired from singles play in 1967 after winning her tenth world singles title.

•

Equipment and Court

It is important to get good equipment in badminton, just as it is in other sports. Buy the best you can afford; it will benefit your play.

RACKETS

Racket prices vary greatly. A tournament player will pay around $20 for a racket, while complete outdoor sets of four rackets, shuttles, net, and net posts can be purchased in some stores for $4. Obviously, the latter set is only for limited recreational activity. Schools will usually purchase a medium-priced racket for their activity classes.

The player who wishes to play a good game of badminton will purchase a metal or wood frame racket (see Fig. 2.1). The laws of badminton do not lay down any regulations concerning rackets. Normally, rackets are about 26" long and vary in weight from 3¾ up to 5½ ounces. They will be strung with gut or nylon, depending upon the preference of the player. Most players who use the wood frame use gut because of its resiliency and "playability." These rackets, if strung tightly, must be kept in a press in order to prevent warping. Those who use the relatively new metal rackets use either gut or nylon. The advantage of nylon in these frames is that it can be strung more tightly than gut and has a longer life. These rackets need no press, since they do not warp.

2

Some players, however, do not like the lightness of the metal rackets. Select your racket on the basis of balance, size, type of grip, whip, and tension of the stringing, rather than "looks."

SHUTTLECOCKS

The shuttlecock, or *shuttle* as it will be called in this book, is manufactured in two different types. The most expensive but also the best for tournament play is the feather shuttle. It is made of goose feathers, weighs from 73 to 85 grains, and has 14 to 16 feathers. The average shuttle for most heated courts is 76, but the room temperature will determine the grain of shuttle used. In a cold Canadian court (many are not heated), you might use 83 or 85 grains, whereas the Malaysians, with their warm, humid climate, would probably use a 73 or 74 grain shuttle. These shuttles cost from $.60 to $.80 a piece. They should be stored in a damp area in order

Figure 2.1 Metal and wood frame rackets with nylon and feather shuttles.

to keep the feathers moist, which will eliminate a lot of breakage. These shuttles will last from one "hit" up to two or three games before breaking up.

The nylon shuttle has become popular in recent years because of its durability and modest cost. Many schools use this shuttle as it costs about $.40 to $.50 and lasts up to two to four weeks for activity classes. It has been accepted as official for some minor tournaments, but is difficult to control for the tournament player who has grown up using feather shuttles.

COURT

The official court in badminton is shown in Figures 12.1A and B (see Chapter 12), giving the singles and doubles court. The net is 5'1" at the net poles and 5' in the center. Law 1(a) states that the lines of the court must be 1½" wide. These lines can be either painted or taped on the floor. Games can be played outdoors as well as indoors, but practically all tournaments to this date are played indoors, where the shuttle will not be affected by the wind. When played indoors, the ceiling should be above 25', although occasionally tournaments are played on courts with ceilings of around 20'. This lower height reduces the kinds of shots possible, as defensive clears and high deep serves cannot be used. Most courts for national and international play are over 30' in height.

Lighting can be a problem. If possible, try to use courts where there are no lights directly over the court which could blind a player momentarily as he looks up to hit the shuttle. In the United States, where most of our play is in school gyms or YMCAs, this is not practical, as we must play in whatever lighting is present.

Basic Skills

This is probably the most important chapter in the book, for you must have good fundamentals before you can develop any advanced techniques. Know and understand this material well before progressing to the next chapter. Each of the strokes analyzed in this chapter will be presented in the following manner: (1) a preliminary skill evaluation will be given—to see what your ability is at the present time; (2) you will read the written material—to help you develop a better understanding of this particular area; (3) several *key points* will be given—which will stress the main components of this skill; (4) a knowledge test will be given—to see if you recall the key points adequately; (5) practice will be devoted to the skill—to develop a kinesthetic feel for the activity; (6) a final skills test will be given—which will measure your degree of skill after the presentation of material and practice. Your preliminary skills test and your final test will be self-administered. All you will need is ten shuttles (if possible), one racket, and either a piece of chalk or several pieces of tape approximately 20' long. You can test yourself at any time you wish to find out your degree of progress.

The basic skills in badminton can be divided into four areas: (1) grips and services; (2) forehand overhead strokes; (3) backhand overhead strokes; and

(4) underhand strokes. Obviously there are other strokes which could be included, but the author feels that it is possible to play a fair game of badminton if you can execute these basic skills. Later chapters will discuss intermediate and advanced skills in stroking.

Several books on badminton stress *wrist snap* as an important part of the badminton stroke. The following phrase has been used on several occasions to denote the difference between badminton and tennis strokes: "Use little wrist in tennis — lots of wrist snap in badminton." This is a poor phrase, for we rarely "snap" the wrist in executing any stroke. The basic reason for this is that the wrist has very little strength in it. You can test this by making a fist and squeezing hard. Where are the muscles tightening up? In your forearm! When someone tells you to build up your wrist for athletics, you can't build your wrist for there are no muscles to build; rather, you strengthen the forearm muscles. In looking for strength, then, don't look at an athlete's wrist size, but look at his forearms.

All badminton strokes are made with *forearm rotation* rather than wrist snap. Granted, the wrist will rotate along with the forearm, but not in the classic action as described and shown in some books. Every stroke in badminton is made with this rotation movement of the forearm and wrist. See Fig. 3.1, which shows the ways you use this forearm rotation on overhead forehand strokes and underhand forearm rotation on the deep serve.

Don't misunderstand! There is some wrist snap along with the rotation, but without the rotation your wrist snap will not have the power to hit even a good clear, much less a hard smash!

GRIPS AND SERVICES

Grips

There are three grips which may be used in playing badminton: (1) forehand; (2) backhand; and (3) *frying pan*. The forehand grip may be used to the exclusion of the others, as some players find they can execute all the strokes without changing their grip at all. Most players, however, do change the thumb slightly to what we call the backhand grip. Each of the three grips will be explained below, but first there are a few points basic to all: (1) do not hold the racket with the fingers bunched together (see Fig. 3.3); (2) hold the racket firmly but not too tightly; and (3) make the racket an extension of the arm.

Figure 3.1
(a) Forearm rotation of deep serve demonstrated by Jim Poole.

(b) Overhand rotation of forearms and wrist.

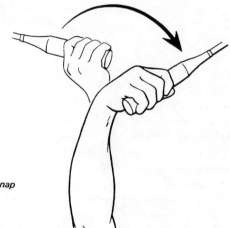

Figure 3.2 The wrong way to *snap* the wrist.

Forehand. Hold the racket by the throat in your left hand with the racket face at right angles to your body. Place your right hand on the strings and slide that hand down the shaft and handle until the center of the heel of the hand rests on the butt-end of the handle. The racket should be lying across the palm and fingers of the right hand (see Fig. 3.3). The forefinger should be separated a little from the others and look like a trigger finger on a pistol. The thumb will wrap naturally around the left side of the handle. All the fingers are spread slightly. This grip is called the *pistol grip* and closely resembles a handshake. (See Fig. 3.4A.)

Figure 3.3 The wrong way: The racket should lie across the palm and fingers.

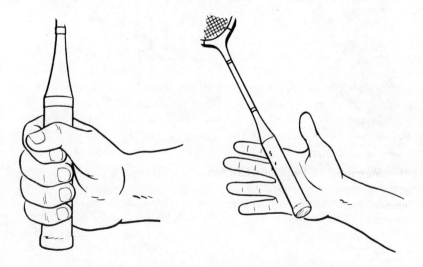

Backhand. The only change in the backhand grip from the forehand is that the thumb is moved from the wrapped-around side position to a more straightened position on the upper left corner of the handle. This allows you to use the *inside* part of the thumb as leverage when rotating the hand and forearm on a backhand stroke. (See Fig. 3.4B.) Some teachers advocate the *thumb-up* grip for backhand shots with the racket turned one-fourth of a turn to the right and the thumb placed flat on the handle (Fig. 3.4c). This particular grip is very effective for beginners as it gives them a little extra power with the thumb flat against the handle. This author does not use this grip, however, for you cannot hit a backhand shot effectively when the shuttle gets behind the body toward the baseline.

Frying Pan. This grip is used primarily in doubles play for serving, serve returns, and net play where only a short stroke is needed. *Do not* use this grip for singles play, as the grip is shortened and only a forehand stroke can be made effectively without changing the grip. Lay the racket on the floor and pick it up with the face parallel to your body. The racket should feel like a frying pan or hammer. The butt of the racket will extend an inch below the palm. This grip is not illustrated in the book.

Services

A Legal Service. Law 14(a): "It is a fault: if in service, the shuttle at the instant of being struck be higher than the server's waist, or if any part of the head of the racket, at the instant of striking the shuttle, be higher than any part of the server's hand holding the racket." (See Fig. 12.2 in Chapter 12.)

For the above reasons, the serve in badminton must be made upward and becomes a defensive shot rather than an offensive weapon, as is the tennis serve. Legally, it can be played either forehand or backhand, although forehand is the usual method. In major tournaments, particularly national tournaments or Thomas or Uber Cup action, an official is used as a *service judge* for every match. It is his duty to enforce the above laws. If a participant violates one of these rules, a fault is called and the player loses that particular service.

Movement of the Feet. Law 16 states: "The server and the player served to must stand within the limits of their respective service courts (as bounded by the short and long service, the center, and side lines), and some part of both feet of these players must remain in contact with the

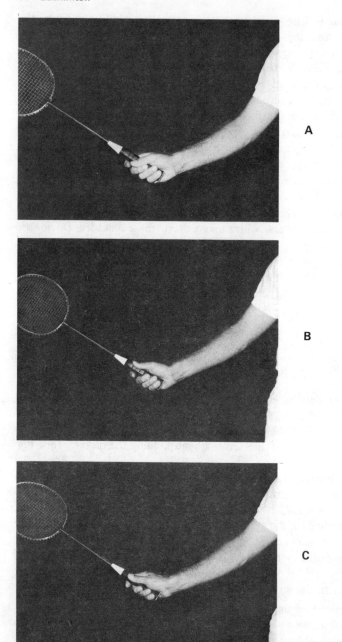

A

B

C

Figure 3.4 Backhand grip.

ground in a stationary position until the serve is delivered." (See Chapter 12.) The service judge is responsible for watching the server's feet and the umpire is responsible for the receiver. If either one moves illegally, a fault is called.

In Proper Court. Rule 16 also states: "A foot on or touching a line in the case of either the server or the receiver shall be held to be outside his service court." This is especially important in doubles to keep the receiver stationary and not moving across the short service line until the shuttle is struck. This rule does not apply to any partners of server or receiver. They may stand anywhere they wish with the following exception, since Rule 16 lastly states: "The receptive partners may take up any position, provided they do not unsight or otherwise obstruct an opponent." By *unsight*, the rule means that your opponents must be able to see clearly the entire service. (See Chapter 12.)

Deep Singles Service (High). Before reading the written material go to the badminton court and take a preliminary test on the deep singles serve. Draw a line (or place a tape) on the left side of the court across the net from you. This line should be approximately halfway between the deep doubles service line and the short service line (see Fig. 3.5); it need not be extremely accurate for this test. Now stand in your right-hand court and, hitting diagonally, serve your ten shuttles underhand. How many did you get in the area between the baseline and the deep doubles

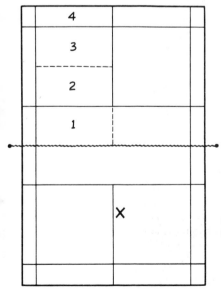

Figure 3.5 Preliminary test: deep singles serve.

service line? How many between the deep doubles service line and your chalk or tape mark? Between the chalk and the short service line? How many did not go over the net? Do not count any that do not go into the left court on the opposing side. If you counted points for these areas (see Fig. 3.5), how many points did you make? A good score for ten shuttles would be between 30 and 40. A fair score would be between 20 and 30. Below 20 is not too good! Do not let it get you down if you scored badly, for if you could serve well on these tests, why read this chapter? Now proceed to the written material.

The high deep serve is very important in singles as it immediately forces your opponent to make a good shot in order to regain the offensive. If he doesn't, you can then attack him. Take a position approximately 3–4' back of the short service line, with the left foot forward. Stand comfortable with the feet spread between 12" and 15" apart and your weight mostly on the right foot. In this starting position, the left shoulder should point toward the receiver. The racket should be held about waist high behind you and with wrist cocked. Hold the shuttle at the base between the thumb and forefinger and extend your left arm out at about shoulder height so the shuttle can be *dropped* (do not toss it) well ahead of the body. (See Fig. 3.6.)

As the shuttle is dropped from the left hand, the racket is swung down and forward. The weight shifts from the back foot to the front foot as the body is rotated to the left, so that at contact point, the body faces the direction of the shuttle's flight. The wrist will uncock to a straightened position at contact point, which should be ahead of the body and between knee and waist level. There is a rapid inward rotation of the forearm and wrist after contact. Follow through of the racket's head should be high and over your left shoulder. Beginners will occasionally wait too long to release the shuttle and bring the racket up to the shuttle before it is dropped. This usually results in a wood shot or a complete miss. The dropping of the shuttle and the starting of a forward swing with the racket should be essentially simultaneous. After you contact the shuttle, step across and straddle the center line. This is the *base* to which you should attempt to return after each shot. Figure 3.18 shows the trajectory of a good high deep serve.

Key Points for the Deep Singles Service:

1. Take a comfortable stance, with most of the weight on the back foot.

2. Extend left arm and drop shuttle before starting racket forward.

3. Rotate shoulders and hips as weight shifts to front foot.

Figure 3.6 Deep single service demonstrated by Judi Kelly, current U.S. No. 3 ranked player in mixed doubles.

4. Wrist and forearm should be rotating as contact is made.

5. Follow through high and extend the arm over the left shoulder.

6. Do not pick up or slide either foot until after shuttle has been struck.

7. Aim for height and distance.

8. Do not push the shuttle—hit it!

Now that you have finished reading the material and key points, how much do you remember? Name the *six key points* (in your own words) which relate to the body mechanics of hitting a deep serve. Name the other *two points* which relate to ideas you should mentally stress while executing this skill. If you cannot write these key points in reasonable form and clarity, do not progress to the next stage of development in this skill. You must understand and know these key points for practice to be meaningful. Reread these points until you know them well.

Assuming that you understand the written material, *practice* should be devoted to perfecting this skill. Take as many shuttles as you can and hit deep serves until you can visualize the proper mechanics and trajectory needed.

Now go back to the court for your final skills test. Use the tape or chalk and mark lines according to Fig. 3.7. The last line should be 2" past the end of the court. This is to encourage deep serves which most players would not let drop during a game. Successive lines into the court from this back line are to be 1' apart. The "A" on the diagram indicates the spot where most opposing players would stand to receive service. Your serves should be hit high enough to be over an average person's reach with his racket extended at that point. The points are scored according to the diagram. A good score for ten shuttles would be between 30 and 40; fair would be between 20 and 30, and below 20 is not very good. Reread the key points and practice on this skill until you can score above 20, for the ability to get the serve deep is very important in singles.

Short Doubles Service (Low). Most players use a short low serve in doubles because of the difference in service courts. In singles you can serve to the back line, which is all of the 22' on the opposite side of the court, but in doubles you must serve to an area shortened at the back by 2½'. Occasionally teams will serve high in doubles, but only if their low serves are not adequate and they have a good defense against smashes.

Normally in doubles you would stand a little closer (about 1' to 2') to the short service line than you would in singles, for the server is responsible for all net shots if he serves low. The rule on service which reads "racket head above hand," is often infringed upon, many times unknowingly. Figure 12.2 from Chapter 12 shows the correct and incorrect ways to serve.

Before reading the written material, go to the badminton court and take a preliminary test on the low service. Draw (or tape) lines on the left side of the court across the net from you. There should be three lines drawn 6" apart on the court starting at the short service line (see Fig. 3.8). Now stand in your right-hand court and, hitting diagonally, serve ten shuttles underhand. A good score would be between 25 and 35. A fair score would be between 15 and 25. Below 15 would not be very good. Now proceed to the written material on low serves.

The starting position is very similar to the one in singles, except the racket is not usually taken as far behind the body and the left hand does not hold the shuttle as high. (See Fig. 3.9.) It is usually held quite a bit lower, so there is not a great time lapse between dropping the shuttle and striking it.

The shuttle should be contacted close to waist level and slightly more to the player's right than in the singles serve. The shuttle is guided over the net, rather than hit. It is a gentle sweeping motion made with the wrist still in a cocked position. There are two reasons for not uncocking

Figure 3.7 Final skills test: deep singles serve.

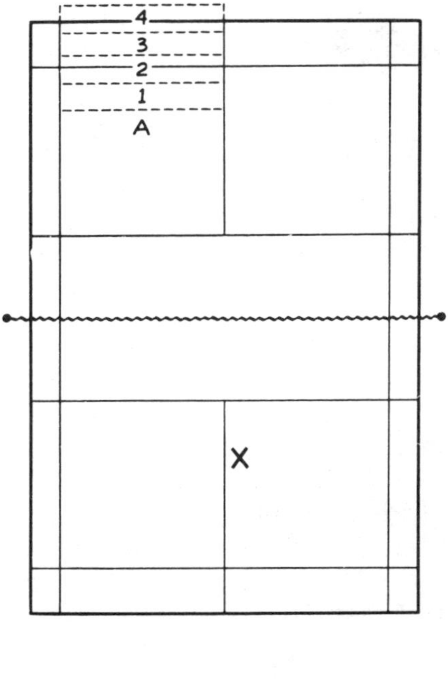

Figure 3.8 Preliminary and final skills test: low doubles serve.

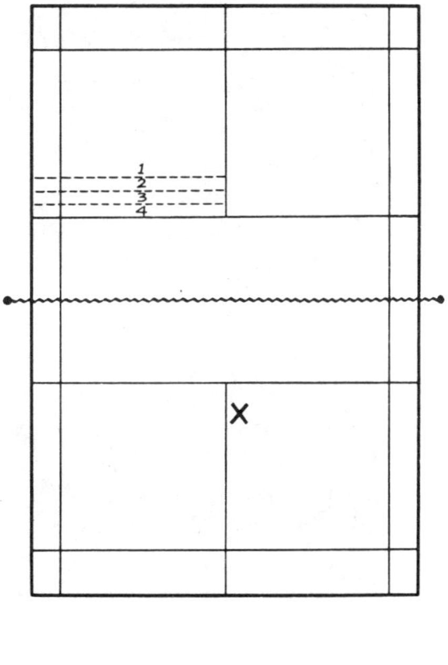

the wrist: (1) if you hit with the wrist, you lose control and the shuttle might pop up over the net where your opponent could kill it (the shuttle travels only a short distance and does not need the power of the wrist); and (2) by keeping the wrist cocked, the threat of a *flick* serve is left in reserve.

The shuttle should reach its maximum height just before reaching the net tape and commence to fall as it goes over the net. A good serve will land within the first 6" past the short service line. The weight will shift from the right to left foot just before the shuttle is contacted, and very little follow through or body rotation is needed. Figure 3.18 shows the trajectory of a good low serve.

Key Points for the Short Doubles Service:

1. Hold the shuttle at chest height.
2. Contact the shuttle slightly below the waist.
3. Guide the shuttle, do not flip it!
4. Keep the wrist firm and in a cocked position during the swing.
5. The shuttle should start downward immediately after crossing the net.
6. Do not move either foot until shuttle is contacted.

Figure 3.9 Starting position of the low doubles serve.

Now that you have finished reading the material and key points, how much do you remember? Name the *six key points* (in your own words) which relate to the body mechanics of hitting the short doubles serve. If you cannot write these key points in reasonable form and clarity, do not progress to the next stage of development in this skill. You must understand and know these key points for practice to be meaningful.

Assuming that you understand the written material, *practice* should be devoted to perfecting this skill. Take several shuttles to the court and hit short serves until you can visualize the proper mechanics and trajectory needed.

Go back to the badminton court for your final skills test on the short doubles service. Figure 3.8 gives the court markings, which are exactly the same as the preliminary test. The only change is to take a piece of cord or rope and tie it 1' higher than the net. All your serves (to count points) must go between the rope and the net. This is to force you to hit good low serves which could not be smashed by your opponents. A good score for ten shuttles would be between 30 and 40, and a fair score between 20 and 30. Below 20 means you need more practice. Reread the key points and practice if your score was not above 20.

OVERHEAD STROKES

Forehand Mechanics of the Overhead Strokes

The forehand overhead stroke, as illustrated in Fig. 3.10, will usually be made from the back half of your court and on the forehand (right) side of the court. First take your *ready position*, which is with feet and shoulders parallel to the net, racket held with grip at waist level and racket head around shoulder level, racket held slightly on the backhand side, with knees bent (see Fig. 4.1). This position is about 4' to 5' behind the intersection of the short service line and the center service line (this intersection is commonly known as the "T"). As the shuttle is hit up to your forehand side, turn your body so that your feet are perpendicular to the net and your left shoulder is pointing to the net. Shift your weight to the back foot and, if necessary, skip backward until you are slightly behind the flight of the dropping shuttle (see Chapter 4 on footwork). This is your *hitting stance.*

As you move backward, the racket arm is raised, wrist cocked, and racket held behind head and shoulders, racket head down, right hand close to right ear. As the stroke is made, several things happen very quickly: (1) your weight shifts from the right to the left foot as the torso is rotated, so that you are facing the target area as the stroke is made; (2) there is an upward extension of the arm led by the elbow, and inward rotation of forearm and wrist; (3) at contact point, the wrist has uncocked naturally so that the arm is fully extended (but not locked) with straight wrist and face of racket flat to target area; (4) racket makes a swishing noise at shuttle contact; and (5) the racket head points downward with wrist at chest level as complete rotation is made — follow-through is across body to left side. This swing can be compared to throwing a ball, as the mechanics are identical. Those same mechanics are used for the three strokes of clear, drop, and smash. You should strive to make all three strokes look the same. This will make your shots deceptive, as your opponent cannot tell what stroke you are playing until the shuttle has been struck. The differences among these three strokes are in terms of: (1) contact point; (2) speed of rotation; and (3) angle shuttle leaves the racket.

Forehand Clear. Before reading the material on the forehand clear, go to the court and take a preliminary test. The idea is to hit the shuttle high and deep into the opposing court (see Fig. 3.18 for proper trajectory of a clear). Draw a line across the width of the court halfway between the short service line and the deep doubles service line. Stand between the baseline and the deep doubles service line on your side ("X" on Fig. 3.11). With your right foot on the baseline, place the shuttle on the forehand side of the racket face with the feathers down. Toss the shuttle overhead, cock the racket, and stroke the shuttle as deep in the opposing court as possible. After tossing the shuttle you can step forward with the left foot as the swing is made. Before taking the test for score, take five practice hits to get used to tossing the shuttle overhead to a good height. Now hit the ten shuttles for score. A good score would be between 20 and 30, a fair score between 10 and 20, and below 10 would be poor.

Be sure to hit the shuttle with the racket face tilting *upward*, for the shuttle will come off the racket 90° (perpendicular) to the face of the racket. Do not let the shuttle get behind you—play it slightly in front of your body. Hit the clear high enough to clear your opponent's extended racket and fall straight down (perpendicular) to the floor. Contact shuttle as high as possible (but be comfortable—do not strain to reach high because it will be an unnatural stroke for you!). Shuttle should land as close to the back line as possible. Use plenty of forearm and wrist rotation to get the shuttle to the back of your opponent's court.

Key Points for the Forehand Clear:

1. Hit the shuttle with an upward trajectory so that it is higher than opponent's extended racket.

Figure 3.10 Correct overhand forehand demonstrated by Chris Kinard, current U.S. No. 1 ranked player in men's singles.

2. Extend the arm upward and contact the shuttle ahead of the body.

3. Keep the racket face flat to the target area.

4. Contact shuttle as high as you can (but be comfortable).

5. Forearm and wrist should be rotating as contact is made.

6. Shuttle should be hit *hard*.

The mechanics of the body are very important in the forehand clear. Can you name the *five key points* (in your own words) which relate to these mechanics? If you cannot, reread this material, for your practice will not be meaningful without a proper understanding of the components of this skill.

Once you have mastered these key points, *practice* needs to be devoted to perfecting this phase of the game. Take several shuttles and stroke forehand clears until you can visualize the proper trajectory and body mechanics needed.

Now go back to the court for your final skills test. Use the same test as you used previously for the preliminary. (See again Fig. 3.11.) Take five practice hits and then ten more for score. Because this is a *clear* test, the

Figure 3.11 Preliminary and final skills test for forehand and backhand overhead clears.

Figure 3.12 Preliminary and final skills test for forehand and backhand overhead drops.

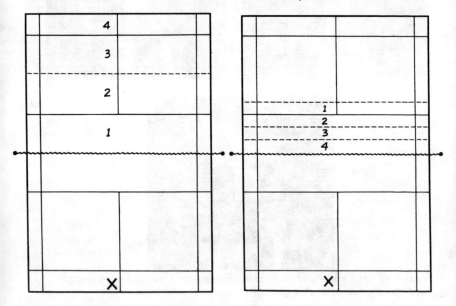

shuttle should be hit upward as it leaves your racket. If an opponent could stand in the middle of the opposing court and reach up with extended racket and touch the shuttle, it is too low. Deduct 1 point for clears that are too low. A good score on the final for ten shuttles would be between 30 and 40, a fair score would be between 20 and 30, and below 20 means you need more practice. Reread the key points and practice on this skill, for this stroke is probably the most important of the shots in badminton.

Forehand Drop. Before reading the material on the forehand drop, go to the court and take a preliminary test. The idea is to hit the shuttle so that it will go barely over the net and land as close to the net as possible. (See Fig. 3.18 for the proper trajectory of the overhead drop shot.) The court should be marked as shown in Fig. 3.12, with the lines 2' apart except for the line closest to the net, which is 2½' from the net. The closer to the net the shuttle lands, the more points you receive. The shuttle should be tossed overhead, as mentioned in the preliminary test on forehand clear, before being struck. Take a few practice hits to get used to tossing and hitting the shuttle. A good score for ten shuttles would be between 20 and 30, a fair score would be between 10 and 20, and below 10 would not be too good.

The drop shot is a slow shot that drops just over the net in the opponent's forecourt, preferably in front of the short service line. Use the same mechanics described under forehand overhead mechanics. At contact point, racket face is perpendicular to the floor or pointing slightly downward. Use full forearm and wrist movement but stroke the shuttle gently and almost push it over the net instead of *hitting* it. Listen to the sound as the racket hits the shuttle. You should barely hear it. This is a good way to practice your drop shot. Try to hit it with *no* sound. Although this is impossible, see how close you can come to no sound. You must follow through on this stroke. Do not hit the shuttle and immediately stop; you cannot maintain accuracy in this manner. Overuse of this shot will allow your opponent to kill the shuttle, as the drop gives him more time to react. Use it, but mix your selection of shots, using smash, clear, and drop in order to keep your opponent guessing. If the shuttle continually goes too deep in your opponent's court, hit the shuttle slightly *upward* so it loops.

Key Points for the Forehand Drop:

1. At contact point, racket face is flat and pointing directly ahead or slightly downward.

2. Shuttle is stroked gently over the net—do not hit it!

3. Hit your drop shot with no sound.

4. Follow through on the stroke—do not stop as shuttle is contacted.

5. To be effective, the shuttle should land close to the net.

6. Loop the shuttle if your shots are continually landing too deep in the opposing court.

After finishing the above reading, to you understand the material and key points? Name *five key points* which relate to the body mechanics of hitting a forehand drop. If you cannot write these with reasonable form and clarity, reread the above material. Do not progress to the practice phase of this skill without an adequate knowledge of the body mechanics involved.

Assuming that you understand the written material, *practice* needs to be devoted to perfecting your skill of forehand drops. Take several shuttles and hit drops until you can visualize the proper mechanics and kinesthetic feel of this stroke.

For the final test, go back to the court and use Fig. 3.12, which was also used in the preliminary. Take five practice hits to get used to tossing the shuttle up in the air off the racket head. A good score for ten shuttles would be between 30 and 40, fair would be between 20 and 30, and below 20 means you need more practice!

Forehand Smash. Go to the court and take a preliminary test on the forehand smash. The idea is to hit the shuttle down hard with accuracy into the opposing court. Figure 3.13 shows the lines and points that you should mark with chalk or tape on the court. Since most smashes are made down the sidelines, only those that land within the two sideline areas will nt on this test. Take a few practice tosses and hits before hitting the s that count. The two X's show that you may stand on either side when you hit the smash. A good score for the ten shuttles would be between 20 and 30, fair would be between 10 and 20, and poor would be below 10.

The smash is the power stroke—the point winner. Clears and drops move your opponent around and eventually force him to hit a weak half court high return. Then the smash is employed as the *finisher* of the rally to win points for you. It is normally not used in the back 2½' of the court (except in doubles) because it decelerates quite rapidly after it has traveled a great distance. Your opponents will be able to retrieve it quite easily if you smash from too deep in your court. The shuttle must be hit downward with as much angle as possible. Angle is actually more important than the speed of your smash, so contact the shuttle from as high as possible. The racket face is pointed downward at contact point and the shuttle is hit in front of your body. The forearm and wrist rotation is very fast and forceful so that the shuttle travels at a rapid downward trajectory. See Fig. 3.18 for proper trajectory.

Key Points for the Forehand Smash:

1. Contact the shuttle ahead of the body with arm extended.

2. The wrist and forearm should be rotating very rapidly as contact is made.

3. At contact point, racket face is flat and pointing downward.

4. Shuttle should be hit hard.

5. A sharp *downward* angle is usually more important than sheer speed.

6. Do not smash from deeper than three-fourths court, as the shuttle slows down very rapidly.

Now that you have finished reading the material and key points, how much do you remember? Name the *five key points* (in your own words) which relate to the body mechanics of hitting a forehand smash. If you cannot write those key points with reasonable form and clarity, do not progress to the next phase of development in this skill. You must understand these key points for practice to be meaningful. Reread any points that you missed until you know them.

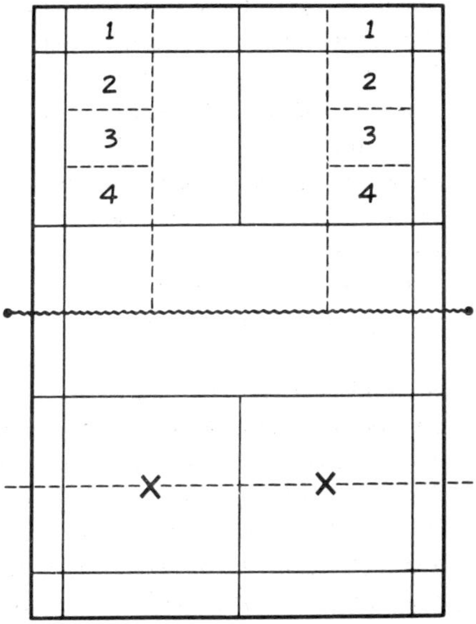

Figure 3.13 Preliminary and final skills test for forehand smashes.

Once these are mastered, *practice* should be spent on perfecting this skill. Take several shuttles and work on this activity until you can visualize the proper mechanics needed.

Go back to the court for your final skills test. Use Fig. 3.13, which was also used for the preliminary test. Take five practice tosses and hits before counting your ten for score. Remember that only those shuttles that land in either sideline area will count. A good score on the final would be between 30 and 40, fair would be between 15 and 30, and below 15 would mean you need more practice. Reread the key points and practice on accuracy.

Backhand Mechanics of the Overhead Strokes

Many players find that the backhand strokes from deep court are the most difficult of all strokes. It requires excellent timing and footwork to hit the shuttle either deep enough on a clear or close enough on the drop for them to be safe shots.

Take a backhand grip for all backhand strokes. The only change from the forehand grip is the straightening of the thumb from a side position to the upper left corner of the handle (see Fig. 3.4B).

From your ready position described earlier, turn so that your right shoulder faces the net. As you get more skilled, you will turn even further and have your back facing the net to hit the backhand strokes. Your weight should be on the left foot, the upper arm angled slightly upward and the forearm angled slightly downward (see Fig. 3.14). This is your starting position. The racket head is pointing downward with the thumb of your right hand pointing to the floor. You'll notice in this position that your forearm is approximately parallel to the floor and the back of the hand is directly in line with the eyes.

Start the stroke by shifting the weight to the right foot. As this occurs, your body will rotate toward the net and the racket will start to extend upward, led by the wrist. A good phrase to remember here is, "pull the racket handle upward." At contact point, the racket arm and elbow are fully extended, and the forearm and wrist have rotated outward so that the thumb is not pointing upward. To get the maximum racket head speed, the hand should stop when the arm gets to the extended vertical position. This allows the head of the racket to accelerate at a faster rate. There is a slight hand and wrist break outward on the follow through. You should get a swishing noise if the execution is proper. Hit the shuttle in front of the body and slightly closer to the net when possible.

Three points should be checked if your execution and results are not satisfactory. (1) Are you extending and hitting *upward*? You must hit up and not forward! (2) Are you sweeping your hand and arm forward like a tennis stroke? If so, you cannot get the timing and power to get good depth in the court, for "you can only accelerate the racket head as fast as you can more your hand forward." (3) Is your wrist in line with your forearm? If wrist is turned *inward* or *outward* at hitting position, the result will be a *sliced* shot. You must keep wrist and forearm in the same plane.

Figure 3.14 Hitting stance and follow through for all backhands demonstrated by Charles Coakley, current U.S. National Junior Champion.

Backhand Clear. Go to the court and take a preliminary test on the backhand clear. Use Fig. 3.11 which was used for the forehand clears, to give you the proper court markings and points. The idea is to hit the shuttle high and deep into the opposing court. Stand between the baseline and deep doubles service line on your side, where the X is on the diagram. With your left foot on the baseline, place the shuttle on the forehand side of the racket face with the feathers down. Toss the shuttle overhead, cock the racket, and stroke the shuttle with the backhand as far into the opposing court as possible. After tossing the shuttle you can step forward with the right foot as the swing is made. Take five practice hits to get used to the tossing and hitting before taking the test for score. A good score for ten shuttles would be between 15 and 25, a fair score would be between 5 and 15, and below 5 is not good. Now go on the the written material.

The grip, stance, and stroke mechanics are the same as listed above. At contact point, the racket face is pointing upward so that the shuttle clears your opponents extended racket and goes deep in his court. To be a good clear, it should land in the last 2½' of the court. This stroke takes good timing, rotation, and racket head speed.

Key Points for the Backhand Clear:

1. Hit the shuttle upward so it is higher than your opponent's extended racket.
2. Contact the shuttle ahead of the body.
3. Keep the racket face flat to the intended target area.
4. Contact shuttle as high as you can (with arm extended).
5. Forearm and wrist should be rotating as contact is made.
6. Do not *sweep* the shot like a tennis stroke—rotate the arm and *pop* it!
7. Shuttle should be hit *hard*.
8. Hit upward and not forward.

After finishing the above reading, can you name the key points? You should be able to name at least *five key points* which relate to the proper body mechanics necessary in learning a backhand clear. Write these in your own words, but go back and reread the above material if you cannot clearly and accurately state the key points. Practice will not be meaningful if you do not understand the mechanics.

Once you master these key points, *practice* with several shuttles to perfect this skill. Be able to relate the practice to the skill you are trying to master.

Go back to the court for your final skills test. Use the same test as you used previously for the preliminary (see Fig. 3.11). Take five practice hits and the ten for score. Because this is a *clear* test, shuttle should be hit upward. If an opponent could stand in the middle of the opposing court and reach up with extended racket and touch the shuttle, deduct 1 point for that clear. A good score for ten shuttles would be between 25 and 40, a fair score would be between 15 and 20, and below 15 would not be too good. Reread the key points and practice this skill if you cannot score at least 15 points on this test.

Backhand Drop. Go to the court and take a preliminary test on the backhand drop. The idea is to hit the shuttle so it will land as close to the net as possible. (See Fig. 3.18 for proper trajectory of the drop shot.) The court should be marked as shown in Fig. 3.12, which was used for the forehand drop. Toss the shuttle overhead as mentioned in the preliminary test on the backhand clear, before it is struck. Take a few practice tosses before taking the test for score. A good score for ten shuttles would be between 20 and 30, a fair score would be between 10 and 20, and below 10 would be poor. Now go on the the written material to learn the proper techniques.

The grip, stance, and stroke mechanics are the same as listed above. At contact point, the racket face is pointing forward toward the net. The forearm and wrist rotation is such that the shuttle is tapped or pushed in order that it may land just over the net. To be a good shot, it must land between the net and the short service line. A common fault is to stop the racket at contact point or shortly thereafter. You must follow through on this stroke. Cross-court drops must be hit harder as they have a longer distance to travel before crossing the net.

Key Points for the Backhand Drop:

1. At contact point, racket face is flat and pointing directly ahead or slightly downward.

2. Shuttle is stroked gently over the net—do not *hit* it.

3. Hit your drop with no sound.

4. Shuttle should land close to the net.

5. Loop the shuttle if your shots are continually landing too deep in the opposing court.

Before progressing to the next phase of development in this skill, how much to you remember of the proper mechanics? Name the *five key points* (in your own words) of the backhand drop. Are they clear and understandable? If you cannot do this easily, reread the above material until the mechanics can be visualized.

Only when you understand these mechanics should you start to *practice* this skill. Take several shuttles to the court and hit backhand drops until the proper swing and trajectory are easily visualized and applied.

Go back to the court for your final test, again using Fig. 3.12. Take five practice hits to get used to tossing the shuttle for the testing. A good score for ten shuttles would be between 30 and 40, fair would be between 20 and 30, and below 20 would mean that more practice is needed.

UNDERHAND STROKES

In general, the stance for all underhand strokes (with the exception of the smash returns) is to have the right foot forward. This allows you to reach a little further, if necessary, and also gives you more flexibility in making cross-court shots. The racket face should be parallel to the floor, with the wrist cocked, and the shuttle should be struck as soon and as close to net height as possible (see Fig. 3.17).

These underhand (or underarm) strokes are usually played somewhere between the short service line and the net. As they are the reply to a drop shot, they are often played below net height and even within a few inches of the floor.

Net Clears

Before reading the material on the forehand and backhand net clears, go to the court for a preliminary test. The idea is to hit the shuttle underhand high and to the back of the opposing court. Mark the court as shown in Fig. 3.15. You should make two lines. The first should be 2½' from the deep doubles service line toward the net. The second line should be 2½' from the first toward the net. Start the test by taking a few practice tosses. Stand with the right foot on the short service line on the right side of your court, where the X is on the diagram. Place the shuttle on the forehand side of the racket head, toss it about 3' toward the net, step forward with the right foot, and underhand stroke the shuttle high and deep to the baseline of the opposing court. For the backhand test, stand with the right foot on the short service line of the left side of your court. The closer the shuttle lands to the baseline the better the clear and the more points you receive. Count ten shuttles each for both the forehand and the backhand clears. A good score for ten shuttles would be between 20 and 30, fair would be between 10 and 20, and below 10 means you had better read the material several times.

Forehand Net Clear. This stroke is almost identical to the singles deep service. The shuttle should be hit high and deep to the back of the opponent's court. As you move to the net for this stroke, the right shoulder should turn slightly toward the net and the wrist should be cocked. Just before contact point, there is inward rotation of forearm and wrist combined with an upward lifting of the forearm. (See Fig. 3.18 for trajectory.) The elbow will finish slightly flexed. You must have good follow through and shuttle must be hit high. Any cross-court clear must be hit harder as it has a longer distance to travel before reaching the baseline.

Backhand Net Clear. The right shoulder must be pointed toward the net and the right foot is forward. The wrist is cocked slightly as the player moves into position for the stroke. Use a lifting of the arm and outward rotation of forearm and wrist to get the desired loft. Elbow again will finish slightly flexed. (See Fig. 3.18 for trajectory.) Shuttle must be hit high and deep to back of opponent's court.

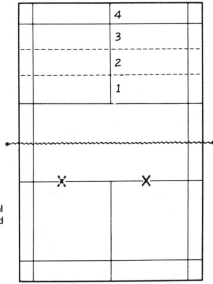

Figure 3.15 Preliminary and final skills test for forehand and backhand net clears.

Key Points for the Underhand Net Clears:

1. Shuttle should be contacted as close to the net height as possible.
2. The right shoulder should turn slightly toward the net.
3. Right foot is always forward (both forehand and backhand).
4. Wrist should be cocked as the player moves toward the net.
5. Rotation of forearm and wrist provide the power to hit the shuttle high and deep (inward for forehand and outward for backhand).

After reading the above material, test yourself on your memory. Name the *five key points* for the underhand net clears. Are they in good form and clear? If not, reread the material, for a knowledge of proper body mechanics is indispensable. If you know why you do a certain movement, the movement becomes more meaningful.

Take several shuttles and go to the court for *practice*. Try to visualize the proper trajectory and mechanics involved in executing this skill.

Go back to the court for the final test (see Fig. 3.15 for marking instructions). Take five practice hits on both forehand and backhand before taking the test for score. A good score for ten shuttles on either the forehand or the backhand net clear would be between 30 and 40, fair would be between 20 and 30, and below 20 is indicative of needed practice.

Net Drops

Before reading the material on net drops, take a preliminary test to see where you stand. The idea is to see how close to the net you can make the shuttle land on a drop shot. Mark the court as shown in Fig. 3.16. Make three lines on the court, with each line 1' further from the net than the last line. Use the procedure for standing with the right foot on the short service line and tossing the shuttle as described in the preliminary test on the net clears. Take a few practice tosses to get used to it, and then hit ten shuttles each in the forehand and backhand for score. A good score would be between 20 and 30, fair between 10 and 20, while below 10 is not very good.

Forehand Net Drop. Use the same mechanics as described earlier for all net strokes. Racket head is parallel to the floor, wrist is cocked, and the shuttle is contacted high. The shot should be gently stroked just over the net. The wrist should remain cocked and shuttle should be struck with a lifting motion. This drop is sometimes called a hairpin drop because of its trajectory (see Fig. 3.18).

Backhand Net Drop. Same as the forehand except the backhand grip is used. Contact the shuttle as close to net height as possible. This gives your opponent less time to reach your return (see Fig. 3.17).

Key Points for the Net Drops:

1. Contact the shuttle as close to net height as possible.

2. Wrist is cocked (and remains cocked) as the shuttle is stroked gently over the net (with a lifting motion).

3. Loop the shuttle so it will land close to the net on the opposing side.

4. Do not pop the shuttle, *guide* it over the net.

Now that you have finished reading the written material and key points, can you relate the proper mechanics of this skill? Name the *four key points* involved in executing a net drop. If you cannot write these four, reread the above material. Know these points well before progressing to another phase of this skill.

Once you can adequately recall these key points, take several shuttles to the court and *practice*. Try to visualize the proper mechanics and trajectory needed in this activity. Only when you can do this should you progress to the next phase.

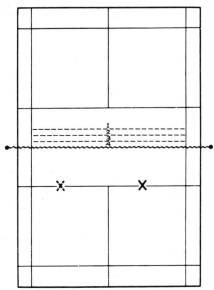

Figure 3.16   Preliminary   and final skills test for forehand and backhand net drops.

Go back to the court for your final skills test. Use Fig. 3.16 for instructions on marking the floor. Stretch a rope 1' above the net on this final test. Any shuttle going over this rope does not count, as an opponent would kill this shot in a game situation. Take five practice hits on both the forehand and the backhand before taking the test for score. A good score for ten shuttles on either the forehand or the backhand net drop would be between 30 and 40, fair would be between 20 and 30, and below 20 means that more practice is needed!

Figure 3.17 Backhand net drop demonstrated by Mike Walker, current U.S. No. 3 ranked player in mixed doubles.

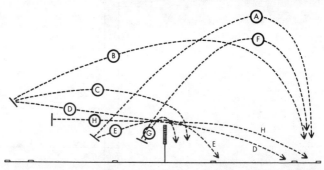

Figure 3.18 Trajectory of the different strokes.

A. Singles (Deep) Serve.	E. Doubles (Low) Serve.
B. Clear.	F. Net Clear.
C. Drop.	G. Net (Hairpin) Drop.
D. Smash.	H. Drives.

Footwork

The object of good footwork is to move as efficiently as possible to all areas of the court. There are six basic spots to which you must be able to move effectively, play your shot, and return to the center of the court. Although you should try to get back to the center of the court after each shot, it is more important to *not* be moving as your opponent strikes the shuttle. If you cannot get completely back to the center of the court, stop wherever you are just before your opponent hits the shuttle.

Each of the six spots will be broken down individually. Footwork is very important, for you can neither hit the shuttle efficiently nor control your opponent if you cannot easily get into position to hit. An important point to remember in badminton is that the last step before the shuttle is struck should always be taken with the right foot (racket foot). This will be emphasized in the material on the six basic spots listed below. Because most players move forward much better than backward, the base or ready position should be 2–3' back of the middle of the court and astride the center line. In the following discussion of footwork, this ready position will be considered as the middle of the court.

READY POSITION

When assuming the ready position, keep the feet even and spread a little wider than the shoulders. The

Figure 4.1 Ready position through movement to left and right front.

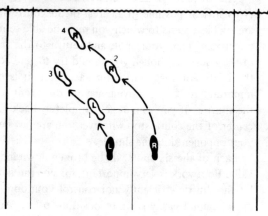

Figure 4.2 Movement to the left front for a backhand underhand net or clear stroke.

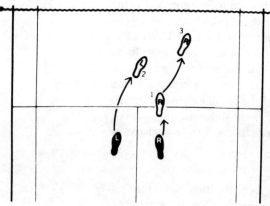

Figure 4.3 Movement to the right front for a forehand underhand net or clear stroke.

knees should be bent with the weight on the balls of the feet. The racket is normally held with its head up and the racket head slightly on the backhand side of the body. (See Fig. 4.1.)

MOVEMENTS

All of the movements indicated below are for a right handed player.

Movement to the Left Front

For a backhand underhand net or clear stroke (see Fig. 4.2).

1. The first step is a small one toward the left front.
2. The second step is a cross-over step with the right foot. The toes of the right foot will point to the left corner of the net. The weight will be over or even in front of the right foot as the racket moves to a ready-to-hit position. The upper body is bent forward from the waist.
3. The next step can be either a long step with the left foot or a short one, depending on how far you need to go to reach the shuttle.
4. Your last step should always be with the right foot (racket foot). Your weight will shift to the right foot as a backhand underhand drop or clear is made. Your feet will be stretched apart with the left foot closest to the center of the court. The hips will lower as the stretch is made and the shot is executed.
5. To return to the center of the court, push off the right foot and move back to the center of the court with small backward steps. Reassume the ready position.

Movement to the Right Front

For a forehand underhand net or clear stroke (see Fig. 4.3).

1. The first step is a long one toward the right front.
2. The second step is made with the left foot in a long step toward the right corner of the net. The racket should be moving into the hitting position and the weight is over the front foot with the upper body bent forward from the waist.

3. The next step can be either a long step with the right foot or a shuffle step, depending on how far you need to go to reach the shuttle.

4. Your last step should always be made with the *right* foot (racket foot). Your weight shifts to the right foot as a forehand under- hand drop or clear is made. Your foot will be stretched apart with the left foot closest to the center of the court.

5. To return to the center of the court, push off the right foot and move back to the center of the court with small backward steps. Reassume the ready position.

Movement to the Left

For a smash return or drive shot on the backhand (see Fig. 4.4).

1. The left foot steps back to set up the line of movement. Your weight will be moving toward the left sideline as the left foot moves back. The shoulder begins to turn so that the right shoulder is toward the net and the left shoulder is back.

2. The second step is a cross-over step toward the left sideline with the right foot. Shoulders are parallel with the left sideline as the racket is brought to the hitting position. If necessary for a longer distance, take a shuffle step.

3. Always end with the weight on the right foot as the shot is executed. Your feet will be stretched apart with the left foot closest to the middle of the court.

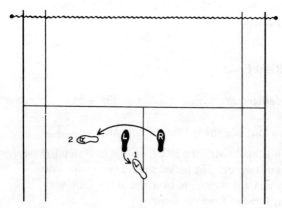

Figure 4.4 Movement to the left for a smash return or the drive shot on the backhand.

4. To return to the center of the court, push off the right foot and pivot on the left foot. Adjust your position in the center of the court with small shuffle steps if needed.

Movement to the Right

Smash return or drive on the forehand shot (see Fig. 4.5).

1. The first step is taken with the right foot. The shoulders turn slightly so that the left shoulder points to the center of the net and the right shoulder points to the back right-hand corner of the court. Your weight should be out in front of the right foot. The knees are bent with the toes of the right foot pointing to the right sideline.

2. The second step is made with the left foot making a shuffle move (left foot moves up to heel of right foot).

3. The last step is always made with the right foot as the racket is brought into hitting position. The feet are stretched apart and the left foot is closest to the center of the court.

4. To return to the center of the court after the shot is executed, push off the right foot and use small shuffle steps to return to the base.

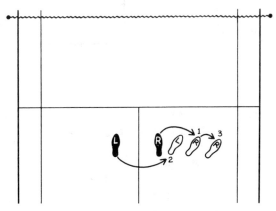

Figure 4.5 Movement to the right for a smash return or the drive shot on the forehand.

Movement to the Back Right

For forehand overhead strokes (see Fig. 4.6).

1. Pivot quickly on the left foot and step toward the back right corner of the court with the right foot. Shoulders should turn so that the right shoulder points to the back right corner.

2. Second step is a shuffle by the left foot to a spot close to the toe of the right foot. The weight stays as much as possible over the right foot.

3. Continue to shuffle with right and left feet until you are behind the falling shuttle near the back right corner of the court. As shot is executed, the weight shifts from right to the left foot. Hips and shoulders turn so they are parallel with the net as stroke is executed.

4. Take short steps to return to the ready position in the center of the court.

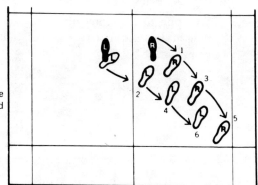

Figure 4.6 Movement to the back right for the forehand overhead strokes

Movement to the Back Left

Backhand strokes (see Fig. 4.7).

1. First make a pivot on the right foot and then take a big step with the left toward the back left corner. Try to step as close to the center line as possible to set up the line of movement.

2. The next step is a cross-over long step with the right foot, which sets up the body in the hitting position for the overhead backhand stroke.

3. As you take another left and right step, adjust your movement to the position of the shuttle.

4. The last step should be taken with the right foot and the toes point to the left back corner of the court. The weight shifts completely over the right foot as the shot is executed and the back will be pointing to the net.

5. To return to the center of the court, push off the right foot, pivot on the left foot, and take small shuffle steps back to the center of the court. Reassume the ready position.

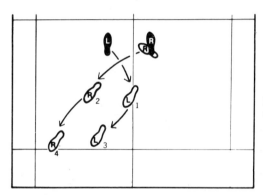

Figure 4.7 Movement to the back left for the backhand strokes

Movement to the Back Left

For round-the-head strokes (see Fig. 4.8).

1. First take a small step backward toward the left corner with your left foot.

2. Next take a backward step with the right foot.

3. Continue to take left and right steps backward toward the back left corner until you can reach the shuttle. (Normally it will only take two steps if you are starting from the center of the court.)

4. The last step backward must be a hop step from the right to the left foot. The shoulders and hips rotate so that the right shoulder and right leg move forward toward the net and the left shoulder points toward the back line. The right foot is lifted in the air for balance. The weight is completely on the left foot. The racket is brought around the head to make the stroke. As the stroke is executed, the weight shifts from the left foot forward to the right foot, and the right shoulder is moved forward.

5. Small steps with the left and right feet are used to return to the center of the court, where the ready position is reassumed.

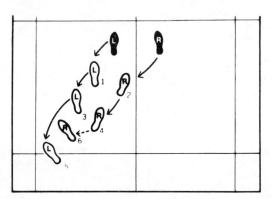

Figure 4.8 Movement to the back left.

In conclusion, try to get back to the center of the court after each shot. If you cannot get there before your opponent starts to hit the shuttle, *stop* and react to where he hits. You can cover a great amount of court if you are standing still and not moving when your opponent hits.

Intermediate Skills

The following intermediate skills have great value when you try to improve your game beyond the beginner level. Each of these skills adds to your repertoire of strokes and poses just a few more problems for your opponent. None of these require any special ability above and beyond the basic skills shown earlier. For example, the drives and round-the-head strokes do not require a change of grip, nor do they require you to hit the shuttle with other than a flat racket. As a matter of fact, the drives are almost identical in stroke mechanics to the overhead strokes, except that they are played sidearm.

DRIVES

The drive is a flat sidearm stroke which is considered an attacking stroke. It is played on both the forehand and backhand sides and is used more in doubles than in singles play. It is probably used the most in mixed doubles, and then only by the man. The contact point for a drive is normally between shoulder and waist height, but it is always hit from as high a position as possible. If hit correctly it will skim close to the net on a line more or less parallel with the floor. (See Fig. 3.18 for the proper trajectory.) The shuttle is struck from the side of the body in a flat trajectory with arm extended and racket face pointing toward the net. Use forehand grip for forehand drives and the backhand grip for backhand drives.

Forehand Drives

The forehand drive is played on the right side of the body and is similar to the baseball sidearm throw. If the shuttle is hit close to you, and time permits, you can use a stance with the left foot forward and shift the weight from right to left foot as the stroke is executed. Normally, however, you will need to reach to a sideline to make this shot. If this is the case, *always* have your right foot closest to the sideline. This allows you more freedom to execute the stroke and return easily to the center of the court.

As the stance is normally taken with the right foot advanced, the racket is brought behind the back until the racket head is between the shoulder blades. The left shoulder points toward the net. To do this properly, notice that the forearm must bend upward, the wrist must be cocked, and the elbow points toward the ground. (See Fig. 5.1.) As the stroke is executed, the elbow will lead the action, which delays the wrist action. At contact point, the following things happen rapidly: (1) the weight should be shifted to the right foot; (2) the body is rotated until at contact point it is facing the net; (3) the arm should be extended; and (4) there should be an inward rotation of forearm and wrist to get maximum timing and power. The arm extension is very similar to the overhead. Try to contact the shuttle to the side and in front of the body (toward the net) when possible. On the follow-through the back of the hand is directly in front of the eyes.

Figure 5.1 Forehand drive.

Backhand Drives

This stroke is similar to the forehand side. Right foot is advanced (usually a cross-over) and the racket is brought behind your body. The right shoulder points toward the net as the stance is taken. The elbow is very important in this stroke, as it must be bent and pointing toward the oncoming shuttle. The wrist is cocked with the palm of the hand facing the floor. (See Fig. 5.2.) As the shuttle is contacted, the following things happen: (1) weight shifts to the right foot; (2) body is rotated toward the net; (3) arm is straightened; and (4) there should be an outward rotation of the forearm and wrist to get maximum timing and power. The follow-through should be toward the path of the shuttle and in the same plane when possible.

Hit the shuttle in front of you.

Figure 5.2   Backhand drive.

Cross-Court Drives

There are only three differences in the swing for all cross-court drives. These are: (1) contact *must* be earlier (at least 12" to 15" in front of the body); (2) rotate forearm and wrist strongly and swing hard, for the shuttle must travel several feet further; and (3) follow-through will be across the body rather than straight ahead.

ROUND-THE-HEAD STROKES

The main values of round-the-head strokes are: (1) you can keep the attack by hitting down, whereas backhands are usually more defensive; (2) they can cover for a weak backhand; and (3) a round-the-head attacking shot from the backhand side, such as a cross-court drop or smash, can be a surprise stroke which might upset your opponent. The big disadvantage of a round-the-head stroke is that you may sacrifice court position if you overuse it, for it causes you to take more steps away from the center of the court to play than does a backhand.

The round-the-head strokes are fairly self-descriptive, for they are forehand overhead strokes played on the left side of the body (the backhand side).

These strokes are usually executed with the forehand grip, although some players prefer to turn the racket more toward the frying pan grip. They feel it is easier to get a flat racket on these shots with this grip. The stroke is closely related to the forehand strokes, except the footwork and body position are quite different. The stroke is started with a forehand stance and the left shoulder pointing toward the net. There is a very quick rotation of the body so that by contact point the right shoulder is pointing the net. (See Fig. 5.3.) The weight is on the left foot at contact point but the player should strive to move forward quickly to the right foot and return to the center of the court. The racket will come around the head and contact the shuttle on the left side of the body. The back must arch and the knees must bend to make this shot. For best results, the shuttle should be contacted above the left shoulder and not any lower. Many players execute a hop to get into hitting position. They will move into hitting position with the left foot advanced toward the net. As the shot is executed, they will hop and exchange feet so that the right foot becomes the front foot. It is from this position that contact with the shuttle is made, and the body starts to shift forward to the right foot and a return to the center of court is made.

To hit this shot correctly, the following points are important: (1) hit with the weight on the left foot; (2) right shoulder and hip must be forward as the shuttle is struck; (3) hit the shuttle at least shoulder high (higher if possible); and (4) do not use this shot if you cannot recover and come back to the center of the court.

Figure 5.3 Round-the-head
stroke

Round-the-Head Clears

At contact point, the racket face points upward and the shuttle is hit to the back of your opponent's court. Most clears of this type are hit straight and not cross-court.

Round-the-Head Drops

At contact point, the racket face points forward toward the net. The shuttle drops just over the net. Either a straight or cross-court drop is very effective, depending upon how your opponent reacts to this stroke.

Round-the-Head Smashes

At contact point, the racket face will point downward. The shuttle must be hit in a downward trajectory. Both straight and cross-court smashes are very effective.

Cross-Court Net Drop

Use the same mechanics for this stroke as for all net strokes. Turn the racket slightly as you start to make the shot (to get proper direction) and stroke the shuttle cross-court. This shot is made both forehand and backhand and must be hit fairly firmly, although very little wrist is used. You must have good follow-through. Do not jab at the shuttle.

SERVICE RETURNS

Since the service must be made upward, you as a receiver should strive to maintain the offensive. As the forehand is normally the strongest weapon of offense, favor it and take all serves in singles or doubles (with the exception of the low serve to the backhand side) on the forehand. If you are not able to attack the serve, make your return to a spot which will put your opponent in the most difficulty. The receiving stance should be with the weight on the balls of the feet, the left foot advanced, the racket head held about head high, and the player ready to move forward or backward as the serve is delivered. (See Fig. 5.4.)

Figure 5.4 Stance for receiving demonstrated by Bob Dickie, current U. S. No. 4 ranked player in men's doubles.

Singles Returns

The stance for receiving singles services should be approximately 5' to 6' behind the short service line, with the left foot closest to the net. Stand next to the center service line in the right court and approximately 3' toward the left sideline in the left court. If your opponent makes a high deep serve, as he will most of the time, skip sideways to the baseline. Be sure to get behind the shuttle, shift your weight forward to the left foot, and execute your stroke. It doesn't matter whether it is a clear, drop, or smash, although there are some percentage types of returns. These are: (1) if the serve is good and deep, clear straight ahead about 75 percent of the time (this forces your opponent to counter with a good shot); (2) smash only when the serve is not deep; (3) drop occasionally to bring your opponent in, particularly if you have been clearing quite often; and (4) do not use a cross-court very often, as it gives your opponent more time to reach it and opens up wide angles in your defense. (Angles will be discussed later under strategy.)

Doubles Returns

The stance should be about the same as in Fig. 5.4, except the location will be about 1' to 3' behind the short service line. The frying pan grip described earlier may be used with great success on your doubles return of service. This shortened grip allows you to move the racket quicker and perhaps block shuttles that come close to you at a fast pace. This is a very valuable asset in doubles play because the shortness of the court on the doubles serve means that most serves will be low. In doubles, meet the low service ahead of the short service line. Racket head should be up, and inaccurate serves should be hit quickly downward. Even if the serve is good and low, play it with the racket head up. This gives your opponents less time to reach your return and also allows you more possible variety in your shots. By hitting down or flat, you maintain the receiver's offensive advantage.

SMASH RETURNS

Rather than breaking down the smash returns individually, a few general points are all that are necessary. There are three returns to learn when a shuttle has been smashed at you. These are: (1) a straight ahead block (just over the net); (2) a cross-court block; and (3) a straight-ahead half court push. The first two are the primary returns used in singles, with the latter used quite frequently in doubles. The returns are made on both the forehand and backhand sides. The right foot should be advanced on both strokes if the shuttle is hit down either sideline and not right at you. The shuttle is stroked gently or just *blocked* if the smash has been hit hard. By a block I mean just placing the racket in the path of the shuttle and letting the power of the smash cause the shuttle to rebound over the net. (See Fig. 5.5.) On the straight-ahead half court push, you must hit the shuttle, trying to make it come close to the net as it goes over so that it will land at about the middle of the court down a sideline.

Most beginners have difficulty with the shuttle that is smashed right at the body. There is no set rule on how to defend on these smashes. Keep the following points in mind: (1) it is much easier to defend on your backhand against body smashes—you have better range of movement than on the forehand; and (2) try to hit the shuttle as far in front of you as you can—do not allow the shuttle to get too close to you, for it will make your return awkward and usually weak.

Figure 5.5   The *block* return of a smash.

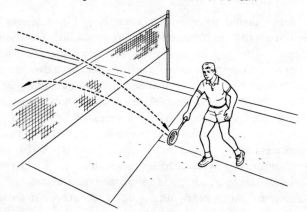

Advanced Skills

There are several strokes in badminton that take a lot of time to perfect before they become a valuable part of your repertoire. Many of those in this chapter may never be learned, but you should at least know that they exist. After you have learned the strokes in the chapters on the basic and intermediate skills, you might want to investigate one or more of the strokes in this chapter.

In all the previous strokes the racket face has been flat to the direction of the intended hit. Many of the strokes in this chapter are hit with the racket face at an angle, which produces a sliced shot. This adds a new aspect to the game—deception.

DECEPTION

Deception is a very important part of the game of badminton, for with its use you can out-maneuver your opponent. Perhaps more deception can be used in badminton than in any other racket game because of the rapid deceleration of the shuttle. Some of the ways deception can be used are: (1) by playing the overhead strokes (clear, drop, and smash) from identical motions up to the last second; (2) by using an angled racket face to slice the shuttle left or right (usually a drop shot or half speed smash); (3) by keeping the wrist cocked and pretending to play a drop (holding the shuttle), then, if your opponent commits himself forward or back, flicking or dropping the shuttle accordingly; (4) by using more or less wrist and forearm rotation to speed up or slow down shots at the last second; (5) by feinting to hit in one direction, then hitting in another (double-motion strokes); and (6) by not overusing a favorite shot or playing in too much of a pattern.

Most deception involves underhand strokes, although you can even hold the shuttle before hitting a clear. An important point about deception and holding a shot is that *it takes time*! You cannot use deception very easily if you are struggling to reach a shuttle. Do not try those feints until you have time to let the shuttle drop before you contact it. Feints or slice shots are very effective against a fast opponent who moves before the shuttle is struck. By holding and flicking, you can slow his pace and force him to play your style of game.

ADVANCED SERVES

Besides the two basic serves (high deep and short low serves) shown earlier, there are two other serves, used mostly in doubles play, that you should learn. If you mix up your low doubles serve with the following services, your opponents must be alert for any situation.

Drive Serve

The drive serve is a fast, deceptive serve which looks exactly like the low doubles short serve until just before contact. It has a low, flat trajectory that is designed to either pass your opponent or cause him to mis-hit the shuttle. The preliminary motion and backswing is exactly the same as the low serve, with a fast rotation of forearm and wrist at contact. Be careful that you do not violate the serving rule. Do not hit the shuttle above the waist. You must, however, be as high as legally possible in order to get the flat trajectory you desire. The best spot to hit the drive serve is at the left shoulder or directly at the face of your opponent.

Flick Serve

The preliminary motions are exactly the same as the low short and drive serves. The main difference is that you will use more wrist action instead of forearm rotation, as little power is needed. The wrist action is used just at contact point to hit the shuttle *just over* your opponent's racket and to the back of the doubles service court. The serve must not be too high or he will get to it easily and smash it. This serve is to keep him honest and not let him stand close to the short service line and rush all your low serves. The best spot to hit the flick serve is wide and deep to the tramlines on the outside of the service area. This forces him to go the longest distance and allows you to get set if he is able to smash it.

Backhand Low Service

This method of serving low has been used for years by the players of Malaysia and Indonesia, but very few Westerners have used it until just recently. The racket is held in a shortened backhand grip. The right foot is slightly forward and the shuttle is held in front of the body with the base pointed toward the racket. The shuttle is stroked gently across the net just as in the forehand serve. Care must be taken to not hit this serve above the waist. (See Fig. 6.1.) Several advantages to using this service are: (1) it can confuse your opponents; (2) it is difficult to pick up the shuttle as it is hidden against your white clothes; (3) it is much easier to hit a powerful flick serve on your backhand; and (4) as it is hit in front of you, it takes less time to cross the net.

BACKHAND SMASH

The mechanics of the backhand smash are identical with the backhand clear and drop strokes. The only difference is that at contact point the racket head must be pointing down, as the shuttle must travel

Figure 6.1 Starting position for a backhand low service demonstrated by Dave Ogata, current No. 4 ranked player in men's doubles for California.

downward. Because you cannot hit it as hard as you do the forehand smash, use it only when you are in the front half of your court. Its value lies in being a surprise weapon, and it is probably used more in singles and mixed doubles than in either ladies' or men's doubles. The reason is that you can direct it to a larger unoccupied portion of the court than usually exists in regular doubles. The speed of the smash is not always as important as the quickness of the smash, which beats your opponent with its suddenness rather than with power.

ATTACKING CLEAR

The clear that you learned earlier under basic skills was a high clear designed to go deep into your opponent's court and which gave you plenty of time to return to the center of the court. It is sometimes called by the name *defensive clear*.

The attacking clear is not defensive! It is used as another weapon in attacking or keeping pressure on your opponent. Used mostly in singles, its height will vary depending upon the size and speed of your opponent. The shot should go only high enough to clear your opponent's racket and then start to fall. This drives him deep into his backcourt. It is especially valuable on certain types of opponents, some of whom are: (1) short players who must go to the backcourt and catch the shuttle about waist high; (2) slow players who let the shuttle get behind them; and (3) players whose centerbase is on the backhand side of the court to protect their weak backhand. (On this kind of player, first hit an attacking clear to his forehand; when he hits a weak return from this, attack his backhand.)

I have seen this attacking clear hit as low as 5' or 6' off the ground if the opponent is short. This stroke is a must for a player who hopes to develop a "pressure" type of game and who tries to keep his opponent under constant control. Both kinds of clears are shown in Fig. 6.2.

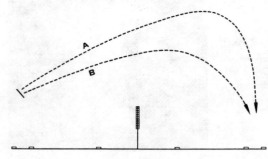

Figure 6.2 Two kinds of clears: *A* represents the defensive high, and *B* the attacking low clear.

ADVANCED DROP SHOTS

The drop shot explained earlier under basic skills is what we consider a slow drop. It travels slightly upward off the racket face. It should land inside the short service line and be hit with a flat face. There are also two other drops which should be mentioned under advanced skills; these are the fast drop and the cut drop.

Fast Drop

This drop is hit quite a bit harder than the slow one (almost like a slow smash). It should barely clear the net and will land beyond the short service line up to 3' or 4' toward the backcourt area. This shot is hit either with a flat face or a sliced partially opened face. Its main values are: (1) in men's or mixed doubles where a slow drop would be killed by a person at the net; (2) to get the shuttle on the floor fast in singles (if your opponent is off-balance or out of position); and (3) as a surprise shot to keep your opponent guessing. (See Fig. 6.3 for the differences in the two drops.)

Cut Drop

This is normally a fast drop and does not usually float across the net. The racket face is partially opened to slice the shuttle. The main values in using this drop are: (1) it is very deceptive as it looks like a straight ahead clear; (2) it gets to the floor fast; and (3) with practice you can control it as well as or better than a straight drop. This slice can be either right to left or left to right. You cannot control the nylon shuttle when you slice it as you can the feather shuttle.

HALF-SMASH

The mechanics are identical with those for the forehand smash in the chapter on basic skills. The half-smash is so called because it has less speed and lands closer to the net. Its chief values are: (1) it does not pull you out of position—after you hit it, it is easier to return to the center of the court;

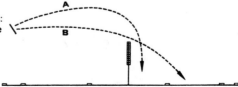

Figure 6.3 Two kinds of drops: *A* represents the slow, and *B* the fast drop.

(2) it is played with less effort, so it does not tire you as quickly; (3) it is good for use against an opponent out of position—it gets to the floor fast (very good for cross-court smashes); and (4) if you are an attacking type of player, it keeps the attack. This stroke can be made with a flat face or a partially opened face (slice). The latter is usually used for this shot. This is used quite frequently in singles and mixed—not as often in regular doubles.

BRUSH RETURN OF TIGHT NET SHOTS

This shot is very valuable when your opponent has played a drop shot from the net which comes over to your right side of the court only 2" to 3" above the net. If you hit in the direction of the net to put it away, you can easily hit the net. Instead, use the forehand side of your racket and swing in the same direction as the net (right to left) and brush (or slice) across the shuttle. (See Fig. 6.4.) This shot will stay in the court because you have taken the speed off the shuttle with the slicing motion. By swinging in the same direction as the net, you also eliminate the possibility of hitting the net, which is a fault. This shot can also be hit on the backhand side of your racket when the shuttle comes over to your left side of the court. The backhand seems to be a more difficult shot for most people, so practice it first on the forehand.

This shot is also valuable in returning a good low serve in doubles. You must catch it at tape level and hit it toward the back opponent on the other team. The brushing action of the shot is deceptive, as it appears to him that you are hitting the shuttle to his right, while in reality it comes to his left.

Figure 6.4   The brush return of a tight net shot.

Tactics
and
Strategy

There is no one way to play the game of badminton. Every year new champions are developing their own successful methods of play. There are, however, general tactics that might benefit most players whether they play a power (attacking) game or a running type of game. In general: (1) be prepared to change your style of play if it is losing; (2) do not change a winning style; (3) develop a "killer" instinct —beat your opponent as quickly as possible; (4) avoid playing your opponent's game—force him to play yours; (5) know that you are fit—this gives you confidence that your opponent cannot "just outrun you"; (6) develop the ability to concentrate and think all the time you are playing a match; and (7) be a champion in defeat as well as in victory.

This chapter will be divided into two parts so that a player can progress at his own pace. The first section will discuss basic strategy for singles, doubles, and mixed, and will be followed by a section on advanced strategy.

BASIC

This section will be devoted to the basic tactics that a beginning player should learn to utilize. Be sure you know the following material well before progressing to the section on advanced strategy.

Singles

Singles is a game of patience, fitness, and court position. Essentially, the basic strategy is to maneuver your opponent up and back by a series of drops and clears until he makes a weak shot or an error. Only when he makes a weak shot do you look to smash for an outright point. Remember that the smash is to finish rallies and not to force openings. If you smash too much it will tire you out, particularly if you are smashing from too deep in the court. Then your opponent can easily defend on your smash and turn it into an offensive shot for him by cross-dropping your smash. It doesn't take very much thought to determine why you run your opponent up and back instead of from side to side. The singles court is only 17' across, whereas the court is 22' long from the net to the baseline. You can run your opponent even further if you make him move diagonally, for then the court becomes approximately 28' long.

It is extremely important in badminton to develop shots for both offensive and defensive play. In every game (perhaps every point of a game), your position will change from offense to defense or vice versa. *Offensive* strokes are those which force an opening or are hit downward, such as smashes, half-speed smashes, drop shots, low serves, and low attacking clears. *Defensive* strokes are those which give your opponent the attack and are usually hit upward, such as high clears (both overhand and underhand), high serves, and underhand drop shots. Drive strokes can be either offensive or defensive, depending on whether they force an opening (offensive) or are hit upward when the cross the net (defensive).

Early in your career you must determine what type of game you expect to play. Are you going to be an attacker, a defensive player, or a combination of the two? Once you make this decision (have a good player or coach help you make it when possible), work on those strokes which are best suited to your particular style. For example, a defensive player would work on high serves, high clears (both underhand and overhand), and slow drops. An attacking player would work more on a mixture of high and low serves, flat fast clears, fast drops, and also hard half-speed cut smashes.

Serve. The main serve in singles should be the high, deep serve. Try to hit the serve so it drops straight down close to the back line, as this forces your opponent deep and, because of the angle, is very difficult to time. Many players will mis-hit the shuttle for this reason. If your opponent is stroking well and giving you difficult shots to reach off your deep serve, it would be worthwhile to try a few low, short serves to upset his rhythm. For the most part, hit the deep serve close to the center line of the receiving court, since this narrows the possible angle of return (see Fig. 7.1). Vary this serve with occasional serves to the outside corners, but remember, this widens the angle of return. Angle of return will be discussed more fully in the advanced section.

Your serving position should be about 3' to 6' back of the short service line and next to the center line. After serving, one step will move you into the center of your court. This is your normal base. Your ready position should be assumed with both feet somewhat wider spread than the width of the shoulders and square to the net.

Service Returns. Your receiving position will be about 6' behind the short service line. In the right court you will be near the center line, whereas in the left court you will be 3' to 4' to the left of it. Be in a diagonal stance with your left foot advanced, as it is easier to move up and back in this position.

If your opponent's serve is high and deep, your best return is a straight ahead clear to the opposite baseline. Occasionally you might vary this with a straight ahead drop shot. Stay away from cross-court returns off the serve unless your opponent has a very weak backhand, in which

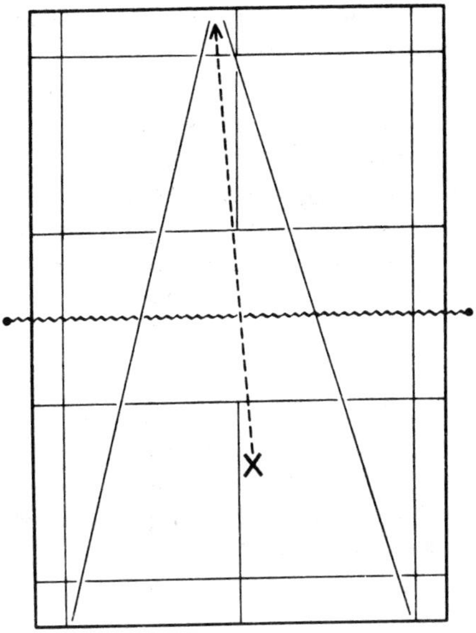

Figure 7.1 A deep singles serve to the middle to narrow angle of return.

case you might clear cross-court to his backhand. If your opponent's serve is high but *short* of the 2½' doubles service line, you can use a variety of returns, such as: (1) smash; (2) cross or straight drop; or (3) fast attacking clear.

If your opponent serves you low, two returns are the most efficient and least risky: (1) a straight drop played close to the net; and (2) a flick straight clear if he starts to move toward the net shot. Always meet the low serve as soon as possible, as this puts more pressure on your opponent.

Do not play too close to the lines in your opening points of the game, as you can make errors. Instead, keep a safe margin inside the lines so as not to present your opponent with gift points. Make him earn each one by putting the shuttle on the floor on your side.

Smash Returns. The best return of a smash in singles is a drop shot (sometimes called a block) to the net. If your opponent has smashed from relatively deep in his court, play your drop about 6" to 8" above the net so the shuttle will loop. This will force him all the way into the net and can turn his attacking stroke into a forcing shot for you. If time permits, play your drop cross-court. This only holds true if he has smashed straight. If he smashes cross-court, play a straight drop. These two drops hit away from your opponent will create problems for him—problems of: (1) time —he has less time to play his next shot; and (2) distance—he must cover more distance before hitting the next shuttle.

General Play. Remember, it was mentioned earlier that your basic shots will be drops and clears to maneuver your opponent up and back in the court. Keep him on the move. Your opponent is more likely to make errors if he must stroke while moving than if he is standing still and hitting.

After every stroke the player should return to the base in the center of the court and be ready for the next shot. This is not always so easy to do. If your shot is a bad one or if your opponent gets to your shot before you can get back to your base, *stop* wherever you are just before he hits the shuttle. Never be moving as he strokes, for you can be too easily faked and fooled. It is surprising how much court you can cover if you stop until the shuttle is struck by your opponent and then move, for you rarely *false step*, that is, take a step in the wrong direction.

When you get into trouble, hit a high deep clear. This gives you more time to get back to your base and helps relieve the pressure your opponent may be applying to you. This high clear can be hit both underhand or overhand and forehand or backhand.

Doubles (Men or Women)

There are three formations that a team might use. These are: (1) sides, (2) up-and-back, and (3) combination. Only the first two will be covered here, as the combination will come under the advanced section in this chapter.

Sides. This formation is probably the easiest to teach beginners (see Fig. 7.2). The court is divided down the middle and each player covers his half from the net to the baseline. The serving and receiving positions on the serve are also side-by-side as during play. The advantages of this are: (1) each player's area is definitely marked and little confusion results which could cause missed shots or broken rackets; (2) it is simple and easy to learn; and (3) it is a good defensive formation and very difficult for opponents to smash through. Unfortunately, the disadvantages may outweigh the advantages of this formation. These disadvantages are: (1) a smart team will play only on the weaker player, running him up and back in his half of the court; and (2) you cannot attack effectively from this formation. Remember this: *attack* is the key in doubles! You cannot beat most teams if you do not attack them.

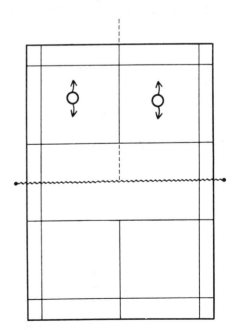

Figure 7.2 Sides formation in doubles.

Up-and-Back. This formation is usually used in two ways: (1) if one partner is quite a bit stronger than the other, the weaker one plays net and the stronger one covers all the backcourt; or (2) if a team wants to try to attack at all times. The court is divided into front and back court and each player covers his half. (See Fig. 7.3.) It is easy and simple to learn and clearly defines each player's responsibilities. The team starts up-and-back and the server follows his low serve in to the net and stays there. His partner covers the backcourt. Its big disadvantage is that the opponents can run the back man from side to side, and it is impossible for him to cover smashes down both sidelines. This is obviously a weak defensive formation. The main advantages are: (1) the ability to attack well from this formation; and (2) the ability to *hide* a weaker player at the net.

There are certain fundamentals which are basic to both of the above formations. These will be covered now, with advanced theories coming later.

Service. The low service is the basic serve in doubles. You do not win very many outright points with it, but it causes your opponents to hit the shuttle up where you can start your attack. The best spot for the low serve is close to the center line, for this narrows the angle of return. In the up-and-back formation, the server must step forward after serving and cover all net strokes. In the sides formation, each partner would cover his side of the court from the baseline to the net.

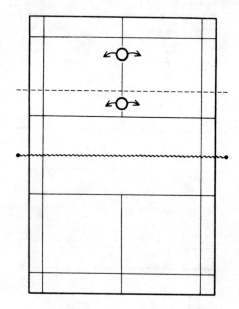

Figure 7.3 Up-and-back formation in doubles.

The flick serve is the main weapon used to offset the opponents rushing your low serve. This serve has been described in Chapter 6. It can be effective when hit either close to the center line or wide to the alley (sometimes called tramlines). In the up-and-back formation, if the server flicks he still goes to the net. He covers only the drop shots, while his partner will take all smashes or clears. In the sides formation, both partners cover their normal halves of the court on the flick serve.

Service Returns.   The receiver stands one to three paces back of the short service line. The stance is covered in Chapter 5. The shuttle must be taken early as it crosses the net and the racket head must be up. Only in this manner can you put pressure on the serving team. Try to return the service with a close drop shot or a push shot down the closest sideline. Avoid cross-court returns, for they widen the area your team must cover. If the serve is high, the receiver should smash the shuttle straight ahead. If he is not on balance, the receiver should play a fast drop straight ahead.

Smash.   The mechanics of the smash are covered in Chapter 3. The position or placement of the smash is very important. Try never to smash cross-court in doubles, as the shuttle decelerates very rapidly as it continues in flight, and your opponent's return can give you difficulty. Your smash should be straight (as a general rule) and to the inside of the man straight ahead. This will usually give him more difficulty in driving the shuttle cross-court where he could hurt you. Another main advantage of smashing in this area is that your partner knows where you are hitting and can anticipate your opponent's return.

Drop.   The mechanics of the drop are covered in Chapter 3. In doubles, the drop is usually not extremely slow, for one of the opponents could anticipate it and kill it. Usually the drop is hit to the center of the court. There are three reasons for using this spot: (1) it cuts down the angle of return; (2) it is easier for your partner to cover the net if you drop in the middle; and (3) you may confuse your opponents as to which one of them is to play the shuttle.

Smash Return.   The mechanics of the smash return are covered in Chapter 5. There are three standard returns of good smashes: (1) a straight ahead drive, (2) a straight ahead drop shot, and (3) a cross-court clear. The disadvantage of the cross-court clear is that it takes very good timing and still leaves you on the defensive. It will be discussed more fully under advanced strategy. The best return of a smash is usually a straight ahead drive down the closest sideline. The straight drive must be hit fairly close to the net and down the alley so that the opponent who covers the net cannot reach it and hit it downward. It must also be hard enough to carry at least past the short service line. This forces the opponent who is in the backcourt to hit it around waist or knee high. He cannot make a strong attacking stroke from this low position. Usually he will play a drop shot to the middle or a flat drive. Either of these should be fairly easy for your team to handle.

If the opponent at the net moves back too deep to try and reach this half court return, you should play a drop shot, either straight or cross-court. The straight drop is safer, usually more effective, and also easier to hit. If you do hit this drop, it is imperative that you follow your shot to the net so that your opponents must hit the shuttle upward, which gives your team the attack.

Mixed Doubles

As a general rule, mixed doubles is played in a manner very similar to the up-and-back formation described under doubles. The man covers all of the backcourt while the woman covers the net. This formation is maintained at all times, if possible. The woman will stand on the short service line during play and during the man's service. The side she stands on during service will depend upon whether her partner is left- or right-handed. (If he is right-handed, she stands on the left side.)

Serve. The short serve is used most of the time. The girl serves from about one pace back of the short service line and follows the serve in to cover all net strokes. The man serves from three to four paces back of the short service line. He does not follow his serve in but stays back and covers all the backcourt. Services will usually be low and to the center of the court, which narrows the angle of return. Because the girl stands closer to the net when serving, the opponents have less time to see the shuttle when playing their return. For this reason most of the points in mixed doubles come from the girl's service. If you have (or can get) a girl who can low serve well, guard her with your life, for she's precious!

Occasional flick serves are good for keeping your opponents honest. They are especially effective in serving to many girls for, even if they get to your service, they cannot smash it through you.

Service Returns. This is a very important skill in doubles or mixed. You must attack the serve to put your opponents under pressure. The receiving stance is described in Chapter 6. Because he must cover the back two-thirds of the court, the man must rush the serve more cautiously in mixed. His two best returns are: (1) drop shot in front of his own partner, or (2) a half court push shot down the closest sideline just past the girl at the net. This forces the opposing man to hit up on his next shot. The girl receiving service can make either a net shot (usually straight) or a half court push just past the opposing girl. Both players should avoid slow returns to the center of the court which the opposing man can drive fast and deep to either corner.

Any high serve or flick serve should be smashed if possible. As a general rule, smash straight ahead down the alley or tramlines. This forces the man to cover the side and hit the shuttle upward. If a drop shot must be made, hit a fast drop straight down the side. Avoid the center of the court with your drop, for the opposing girl should be there to kill any weak drops.

Smash. All smashes in mixed are generally directed down the sidelines, as your opponents are normally up-and-back. More important than speed in your smash is the trajectory. Hit the shuttle down at a sharp angle. Then if it comes back, it must come up to you and you keep the attack. If you do not wish to smash down the sideline, smash directly at the girl.

Drop. As mentioned on service returns, all drops must be fast ones directed down the sidelines away from the center of the court. The man must be careful of drops because he is usually hitting from the back court, and a slow drop can be killed by the opposing girl. For this reason, he normally plays half court push shots past the girl instead of drops. The girl at the net must be able to hold her own playing drop shots with the opposing girl. She should only hit cross-court drops when the opposing girl is pulled over to one sideline.

Drives. Drive mechanics are covered in Chapter 5. The drive strokes are used more in mixed doubles than any other game. Be careful of the cross-court drives. They are probably *overused* rather than underused. Only use this stroke when the opposing players are both pulled to one sideline. Other than the above, keep your drives straight and down the sideline.

Smash Returns. In basic mixed strategy, the girl would duck all smashes and cover only net shots. Later, in the advanced section, she will learn a couple of skills to aid her partner when protecting against a smash. Normally the man will defend against the smash in mixed from about 5 or 6 paces back of the short service line. He tries to keep his return flat and straight down the closest sideline. If he can hit it half court just behind the opposing girl, well and good. But if he cannot, he hits it hard and flat so that the opposing man gets it lower than the net and cannot smash it again. Occasionally, your opponent's smash can be driven cross-court if he has smashed off balance or from too deep in his court.

ADVANCED

This section will be devoted to skills involving more than the basics described earlier. Remember, badminton is a game which requires you to *think* if you expect ever to be a champion.

Learn to concentrate on each point in the game and try not to give any points away without your opponent earning them. Use the warmup session and the first few points of a match to determine what kind of player you are facing. Is he slow afoot? Is he erratic? Is his deep backhand weak? Does he overplay so much to cover his backhand that he opens up his forehand corner? Can you beat him with quick shots? If he has a weakness, find it! Try to win every tournament match with a minimum of effort, saving that energy for those tough matches that will come later.

Warmup. In many tournaments you cannot take 10 to 15 minutes for a warmup, so do some limbering up exercises before you go to the court for your match. Start with shoulder and arm rotations and slowly work down until you have stretched the back and leg muscles thoroughly (see Chapter 9). This will prevent pulled muscles and get you ready to play. During the warmup rallies, aim for specific spots when you stroke so you start gaining the accuracy needed at the outset. Practice the specific strokes which will be needed for the game you are about to play (for example, clears and drops in singles; smashes, drops, and defense in men's doubles; drives for the man and net shots for the girls in mixed doubles). Scout your future opponent if time permits. Note whether he is left-handed, likes to run, smashes hard, and so on.

Advanced Singles

Practice. Every time you go on the court for practice, use your brain. Have a definite goal in mind for each training session. For example, if your smash defense is weak, clear short to your opponent and let him smash. This will give you valuable practice in returning smashes and he does not need to know you are practicing. If you have a partner who will practice with you, well and good. If everyone says, "I do not like to practice, let's play games," do not despair. Use the games to practice certain skills. Occasionally play a game without using one of your basic strokes (clear, drop, or smash). Use only the other two and try to win. This gives you valuable training. Drills that you can use with a willing partner will be discussed in Chapter 8.

In practice, work on hitting the two types of clears: (1) a defensive (high) clear, and (2) an attacking (low) clear. Practice playing one game with all defensive clears. Then play another game and use only attacking clears. Spend a lot of time and effort on perfecting your *length* in the clears. This one item probably causes more losses than any other skill—the inability to hit a good clear that will consistently land within 6" of the back line.

Avoid Stereotyped Play. Be sure you do not get into a stereotyped pattern which your opponent can anticipate. Figure 7.4 shows poor and good variety. Instead, play two, three, or four shots in a row to the same corner.

A Conditioned Response. A good sequence to use against some players is what is called the *conditioned* pattern. Hit four, five, or six shots to one spot and then with the same motion, to disguise your intentions, hit to the diagonally opposite corner. (See Fig. 7.5.) After you have hit four or five to one corner your opponent may get conditioned to this shot and take a step in that direction as you prepare to stroke again. The shot to the opposite corner will beat him.

Figure 7.4 *Poor* and *good* variety in singles pattern.

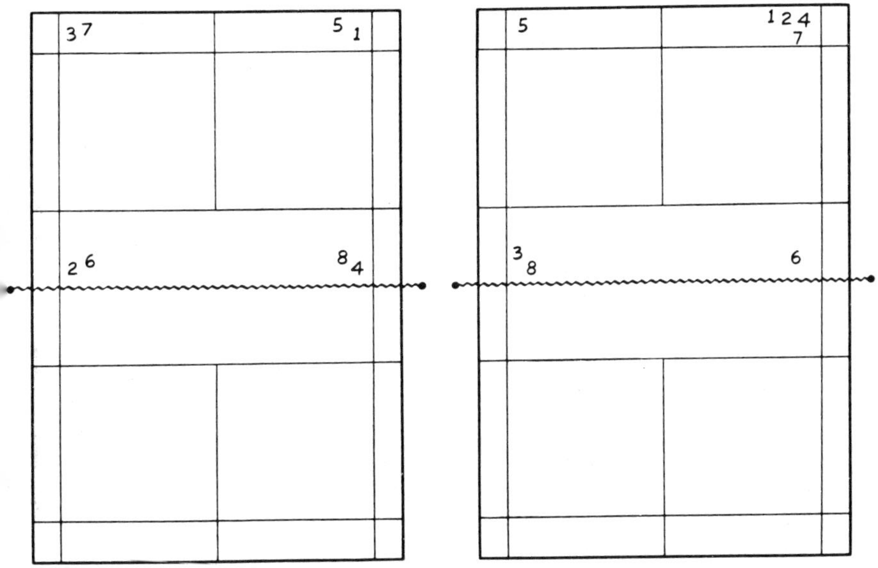

Center Court Theory.   A good strategy to use at the end of a game involves the center court theory. Let's say the score is 12–12, 10–13, 9–14 (and you are losing), and you are faced with the problem of trying to completely eliminate all errors from your game. Under this system you do not hit shots close to a sideline. Primarily you try to smash a lot, using body smashes against your opponent. Change the pace of your smash and change the position you try to attack. If you must clear or drop, hit into the center of the court. This eliminates most errors and narrows the angles open to your opponent.

Body Smashes.   These are underused by most good players today. Most players defend well against sideline smashes, for they are reaching and have full use of the arm and racket. A smash into the body, however, will often cramp their return and force them to hit a drop short or a pop up. As most players carry their rackets slightly on the backhand side, your target should be the right side of the opponent's body. (See Fig. 7.6.) If you hit a good smash, move to the net and kill the cripple which usually results. If your opponent is able to hit a good drop, there is nothing lost, for you are at the net and ready to play your return anyway.

Half-Speed Smashing.   This skill is very valuable in singles. For the most part, this is the smash to hit on all cross-courts, because it forces your opponent to move forward to play this shot or be beaten by the

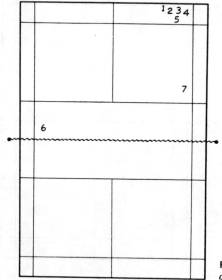

Figure 7.5   A pattern to achieve a *conditioned response.*

angle. Remember that a hard smash will carry the shuttle much deeper in the opposite court. See Figure 7.7 for a combination of hard and cut smashes.

The Power Game. If you have a strong smash and are reasonably quick, you might want to try this type of game. Learn to get the attack as soon as possible in a rally and continue to attack until you win the point. The key word with this style of play is *pressure*. Get your opponent under pressure and keep him there until he cracks. Besides the high deep serve, two others are important for a power player: (1) a low serve, and (2) a flick deep singles serve. The latter is used while you are successfully maintaining the attack with a low service. This deep serve variation keeps your opponent from rushing your low service.

On every occasion when you want to clear *and* are on balance, use the low attacking clear. This shot, if properly executed, gets the low attacking clear. This shot, if properly executed, gets the shuttle behind your opponent, who must then lift the shuttle to you. See Chapter 6 for mechanics of this stroke, which should usually be played straight ahead. It doesn't matter whether you hit it to the forehand or backhand side of your opponent.

Figure 7.6 Target area for body smashes.

Figure 7.7 Two different kinds of smashes: *A* represents the hard, and *B* the half speed or *sliced* smash.

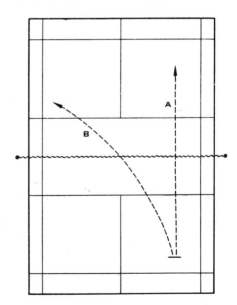

A hard smash is very helpful with this style of play, but more important is proper placement of the smash. Learn to smash straight, cross-court, and into your opponent's body. Varying these three smashes creates more problems for him. The half-speed smash is a necessity with the above hard smash, for there are numerous occasions when you want to attack but are too deep in the court or are off-balance and the hard smash would hurt your court position. Use the half-speed smash on these occasions and keep the attack. The great value of this half-speed smash is the steep angle and trajectory that forces your opponent to come forward in the court to reach it.

Most drop shots should be fairly fast ones so they get below the level of the net quickly. This forces your opponent to hit up. It does not matter if the shuttle carries a little past the short service line on this fast drop.

To play a really good attacking game, you must also develop a good net game. Make your opponent afraid to play net with you. If he is deep in the court and has hit a drop shot, play your return about 5" above the net and let it come down close to the net. (See Fig. 3.18.) This forces your opponent all the way into the net. If he clears from this position, he will not normally be able to get the shuttle deep. If he does clear short, *attack* with your smashes.

Work to get a weak return that you can kill. If you are unable to kill the shuttle when you are at the net, push it quickly into your opponent's body. This usually elicits a weaker return that you can kill.

Angle of Return.   The angle of return is the angle through which your opponent can hit the shuttle. In singles, you try to do two things: (1) narrow the angle to which your opponent can hit, and (2) widen the angle to which you can hit. The easiest method of studying angle of return is on the serve. If you serve from next to the center line of your court to a spot close to the center line of your opponent's court, you narrow the angle and equalize the danger on either side. Your opponent must hit away from you to try and pass you. (See Fig. 7.1.)

If you serve deep and to the sideline, you widen the angle of return. You must cover the straight ahead shot down the line possibility first, but you are then left vulnerable to the cross-court shot. After a serve such as this, move 2' or 3' to the left. Now you are *centrally* in the angle of return. This angle of return holds true on all shots, but it is much harder to adapt your position during a rally than during the serve.

Probably the most misused shot in badminton (which violates this angle of return) is the cross-court net clear after your opponent has hit a drop shot from deep in his court. When you hit this shot, you immediately widen the angle of return. If your clear is short, he can smash straight ahead and beat you, or if you guess and run quickly, a smash behind you will win. For this reason, if your opponent hits a drop shot from deep court and you wish to clear, 90 percent of the time clear straight!

Court Position. Court position will vary depending upon what shot you have hit, the possible angle of return, and what alternatives your opponent has in his selection. For example, if you have hit a good close drop shot and your opponent must come from the backcourt to retrieve it, do not run back to your central base! Wait at the net and, if he plays a net return and it is high, kill it! If he clears, it almost certainly must be short. You will have plenty of time to walk back to half court and smash it.

Many times you can eliminate one or two spots to which your opponent cannot hit. When this happens, vary your court position so as to be close to the probable returns.

Advanced Doubles (Men or Women)

The best formation to play in doubles is a mixture of the sides and up-and-back formations. This is called a Combination (or rotation) System. Because it takes extremely good teamwork, advanced skills are necessary to make it work. This system has simple rules for court positions. They are: (1) when the shuttle is up in the air and you are attacking, be in an up-and-back formation; (2) when the shuttle must be hit up by your team, adopt a sides formation so you can defend. As you can see, your team will be making a constant change (or rotation) from sides to up-and-back and from up-and-back to sides, depending upon the situation. Figure 7.8 shows how this is done most efficiently.

If either player should clear the shuttle while in the attacking formation, the team immediately assumes sides. Since the back line player can see the net player coming back, he assumes the opposite side from that which the net player chooses. Normally the net man would come straight back.

The same change of formation must occur when the defensive team gets a high shuttle and starts to attack. The player away from the shuttle goes to the net, and the player who is closest moves over to smash or drop.

If the shuttle is lifted only to midcourt, it is best if the striker moves forward to the net after hitting it down. This is best for several reasons: (1) he is usually moving forward when he hits anyway; (2) he is moving and thus more ready for the next shot; and (3) since he hit the last shot, he should have a good idea of the opponent's reply.

Services. Reread the material on drive, flick, and low serves in Chapter 6. As mentioned earlier in this chapter, the basic serve in doubles is low. Because most good players will stand close to the short service line and move across just as soon as the shuttle is struck, however, your low service must be varied in placement. Even this may not be good enough against a good net rusher. You must use a deceptive flick or drive serve to fool your opponent; he will not be able to rush as effectively if you have flicked or drive-served him successfully. The preliminary motions of the low, drive, and flick serves must look exactly the same. The proper mechanics of these strokes are covered in Chapter 6.

As previously mentioned, vary the placement of your low serve. Three spots are effective! (1) The *best* spot is always closest to the inside of the opponent's playing court next to the center service line. This narrows the angle of your opponent's return. (2) Another good service placement is wide to the alley. This is effective against some people who do not move or change direction well. Many times the opponents will push this serve deep. If you have served from the left court it allows your partner to drive his return fast and hard. (3) A third spot is your opponent's left shoulder if he receives with his racket held on the forehand side, as most players do! If he receives with the racket on the backhand side, serve to the right shoulder. This spot is very good against an

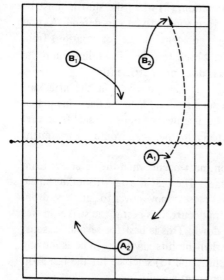

Figure 7.8 Combination formation in doubles.

opponent who has difficulty changing his racket from one side to the other. Many times a player will have a moment of indecision as to which side of the racket to use to play the shuttle, and he will eventually hit a weak return.

The drive serve is valuable against players with slow reactions. It is usually served right at the face of your opponent or to his left shoulder. *Avoid* this serve (to the left shoulder) if your opponent hits a good around-the-head smash.

The flick serve is made to one of the two following areas: (1) to the outside of the court in the tramlines; or (2) to the inside of the service court next to the center service line. Both serves have certain advantages. The serve to the outside takes longer for the opponent to reach, thus giving your team more time to get set for his return. If he smashes cross-court, the server has a slower shot to react to than if the serve is to the inside and a smash played straight ahead. The advantage of the serve to the inside is that it is to your opponent's backhand side and he may be unable to smash around-the-head. He may have to hit up, which immediately gives your team the attack.

Advanced Service Returns.   As mentioned earlier, hit the shuttle as soon after it crosses the net as possible. You should learn several varied service returns. This puts extreme pressure on your opponents just to get the shuttle back over the net, which takes their minds off attacking you. The better returns of service are: (1) a half-court push, usually straight, just past the server but in front of his partner, (2) a straight drive deep to the box in the back corner, (3) a drop shot away from the server, (4) a push shot into the server's partner aimed about chest high on the forehand side (if he defends on the backhand), and (5) a push shot just over the back of the server, who usually steps forward as he serves to cover the net. Two other returns are very effective if the serve is delivered low to the outside alley: (1) a push shot cross-court straight into the server as he moves to cover his serve, and (2) a half-court straight push shot off the serve. This shot should be past the server but in front of his partner. Should your opponents flick serve you, hit a half-speed smash straight ahead. This shot will give the opponents trouble, for it has good trajectory and does not leave you off balance. A drive serve by your opponents should be smashed back at the server or blocked quickly over the net toward the middle of the court.

Advanced Smashing.   The best placement of a smash is *always* to the inside of the man straight ahead, as mentioned in basic strategy. The main reasons for this are: (1) it is more difficult for an opponent to hit a hard cross-court drive, which could hurt you; (2) the straight smash gets to the opponents quicker; and (3) your partner knows where you are smashing and is able to anticipate certain returns from the opponent. Because most players defend better on the backhand, some teams prefer always to smash to the opponent's right side. They feel this forces a weaker return, particularly if the smash is kept close to the opponent's right hip.

If your opponent is defending well against your smash, change the spot of your attack to alternating sides (such as forehand to backhand to forehand to backhand). This forces him to alter his position on each of your smashes. If he retreats deeper in the court to have more time on your smashes, use a steep angled smash with a little less power. This shot may hit the floor in front of his outstretched racket. Vary the speed of your smashes. Occasionally hit a flat, slow smash into your opponent's chest area. This may change his timing and rhythm, particularly if he is having success against your hard smash. If your opponent moves toward the center of the court to defend, smash down the alleys. This is particularly good if you first smash one down the middle of the court to open up this area.

If your opponents lift the shuttle down the center of the court, smash down the center line. This is good for a couple of reasons: (1) indecision may cause neither player to hit the shuttle; and (2) the angle of the opponent's return cannot give you great difficulty as could a sideline smash. *You win in good doubles by smashing.*

Advanced Drops. The basic strategy section covered this area well. The drop is used in doubles for: (1) deception, (2) to gain (or regain) your balance, and (3) as a variation from smashing.

Advanced Smash Returns. The straight ahead drive and straight drop shot returns were covered in the basic strategy section. Three other returns are used frequently in doubles. They are: (1) a cross-court drive, (2) a cross-court clear, and (3) a cross-court drop shot. The cross-court drive is particularly effective when your opponents are both shifted to one side of the court. Be sure to contact the shuttle well out in front of the body when you make this shot. The cross-court drop is also used if your opponents are both shifted to one side of the court and anticipating a straight drive or drop. Remember that this shot is risky if hit too slowly, for it takes longer to cross the net. You must follow this shot to the net as it is hit in order to force the opponents to hit the shuttle upward. If you are at the net, they will be fearful of playing a return drop which you might kill. The cross-court clear must be timed correctly to consistently place your opponent's smash in the back foot of their court. If both you and your partner are good on defense and feel that you might tire the attackers and win in this manner, this could be the style for you. Hit the shuttle well in front of you and be aware of possible changes in shuttle speed, for mistiming can ruin your deep defensive return.

What happens if you are the player cross-court from the smasher? We know that as a general rule the attacking team works on the man straight ahead. As the cross-court player, you must cover smashes to his inside down the middle. Ordinarily you try to hit two returns. These are: (1) a block or drop back to the same side as the smasher, with your partner following it to the net, or (2) a straight drive down your closest sideline. If this straight drive gets past the opponent at the net, it will win a rally outright or force the smasher to make a long run to retrieve it. If he does reach it, he will probably have to hit the shuttle upward, which will give your team the attack. (See Fig. 7.9 for these two returns.)

Advanced Mixed Doubles

Advanced Services. This was covered well in basic strategy. An occasional drive serve or low serve into the left shoulder is also effective. This low serve may cause a moment of indecision regarding use of the

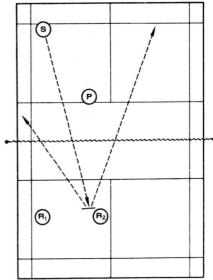

Figure 7.9 Smash returns by the cross-court defender.

forehand or backhand side of the racket to hit the shuttle. In the basic section, it was noted that the girl stands on the short service line when the man serves, and to his *left*, if he is right-handed. Many men, however, will place their girls on the same side on which they are serving. They feel that this gives their team better position in case the opponents hit a straight drop. The man must be careful to give the opponents a good look at the service and not unsight them with a partial blocking of the shuttle by the girl's position.

Advanced Service Returns.   Besides the two basic service returns of the drop shot or the half-cour push, there are three other possible service returns in mixed doubles: (1) A straight flat drive into the "box" where the two side and end lines converge, (2) A push into the man's chest (often cut across slightly to take the speed off the shuttle), which is usually made by the man if he has a strong girl partner who can play behind him so he can rush the net, and (3) A short half-court shot played just over the server's shoulder. **Caution**—Use this only against the girl's serves, for the man has too much time to see the shuttle.

Advanced Smash, Drop, and Drives.   These strokes were covered well in the basic section on mixed doubles. The only problem which ensues in advanced mixed is the up-and-back defensive formation where the girl covers the smashes away from the smasher. (See Fig. 7.10.) This formation poses a problem for the attacker, for if he smashes straight ahead, the opposing man is set for the shot. If he attacks the girl with his slower cross-court smash, it may be picked off and blocked down his opposite sideline. Then what can he do? If smashing is not successful (try it first), try steeply angled smashes to the body or the left shoulder of the girl. If this does not work, use straight drops to bring the man in, mixed occasionally with flat attacking clears over the girl's head, which may cause problems for the opposing man. You should also try smashing or dropping down the center to see if this poses a problem of who will play the shot. Every defense has a weakness—keep probing until you find it!

Advanced Smash Returns.   As mentioned earlier, the man tries to defend against his opponent's smash with a straight ahead half-court drive. It must go over the net low and close to the sideline so the opposing girl cannot reach it. This takes the attack away from the opponents. Occasionally, if the girl moves over to try to cut off one of these half-court drives, a cross-court block to the net is very effective. It must not be too slow or the girl can recover and still hit it down.

The girl can help defend against smashes by the opposing man in two ways: (1) cover all of one side as in regular doubles if she is exceptional; or (2) cover all smashes directly at her on the side opposite to where the smash has been struck. This last formation needs a little explanation. Teams that use this defensive formation, sometimes called a *diagonal defense*, try always to clear down one sideline. This gives the girl time to get cross-court away from the shuttle. The girl stands in front of the short service line with her racket head up. She covers only smashes or drops directly to her side, with the man covering all the other areas. Her partner would cover the straight drops, straight smashes, and clears to his or her side of the court. (See Fig. 7.10.)

When the man smashes cross-court at the girl, she just blocks the shuttle straight ahead. It will usually go half-court past the opposing girl and give the man considerable difficulty. The reason the girl can cover this shot effectively is that the smash hit cross-court must be hit further, and therefore reaches her with a little slower pace than would a straight smash.

Strategy During Play.   The girl's role in mixed is to hit all shots downward, when possible, at the net. She takes a very limited backswing on shots and tries for kills or half-court push shots when possible. She should never reach behind to play a shot, for usually the man is in better position to play the shot, as he has more time. If the girl does reach back, she usually hits a weak return. She must be a very accurate net player and have the confidence to play the opposing girl at the net. She keeps these

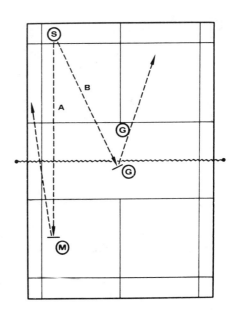

Figure 7.10   Smash returns of an up-and-back mixed doubles team: *A* (man) blocks smash straight to one-half court, *B* (girl) blocks smash down opposite sideline.

shots straight unless the opposing girl has been pulled to one side of the court, in which case a cross-court drop can safely be played.

The man in mixed doubles will usually hit about two-thirds of the shots. He keeps the shuttle flat (or downward) when possible with half-court drives. If the opposing man gets to your half-court fast and is giving you considerable difficulty with his returns, play deep into the corner boxes. This gives him less time to fake you. See Fig. 7.11 for a sample rally with a good mixture of shots by the man that keep his opponent off balance. Whenever the opportunity presents itself, a team should *smash*, for this will win in doubles or mixed.

If you play against a mixed doubles team that plays the sides formation, attack them like regular doubles by hitting your smashes and drops down the middle. If the opposing girl is not strong, use drops and attacking clears to move her up and back in the court. Occasionally the man will be weaker, so you should move him up and back with clears and drops until a weak return can be smashed for the point.

Figure 7.11 *Good* pattern of shots by the man in mixed doubles.

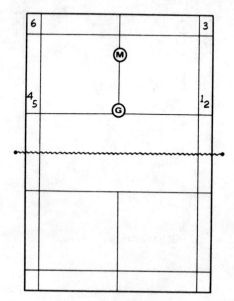

Drills
and
Games

This chapter will be divided into two sections: basic drills and games, and advanced drills and games. This is done so the player can progress at his own pace. Once he has conquered the basic section adequately he should move on to the advanced.

Why spend time on practice which could be spent playing games? Psychology has shown us that overlearning needs to take place before a person can execute motor skills correctly. You must practice a particular skill until it becomes a part of your neuromuscular pattern. The racket must feel natural in your hand, and the contact between the racket head and the shuttle must be coordinated to permit good timing and proper stroking.

BASIC

Overhead Clear Drill

Both players (A and B), as illustrated in Fig. 8.1A, start from the center of the court, with A using a deep singles serve to get the rally going. B clears it back with an overhead clear. The object is to clear the shuttle high and deep back and forth across the net. Work first on straight clears and use only forehand or round-the-head overhead strokes. After you become proficient at hitting forehands, work also on the overhead backhands. Once you are able to clear straight consistently to within 1' of the back line, then work on cross-court clears along with the straight ones. Because of the increased distance when you hit cross-court, be sure to hit the shuttle harder.

Overhead Dropshot and Underhand Clear Drill

Both players (*A* and *B*), as illustrated in Fig. 8.1B, start in the center of the court. *A* starts the rally by a deep serve and *B* returns the serve with an overhand drop shot, trying to keep the shuttle inside the short service line on his opponent's side of the court. *A* will move forward and return this drop with a high clear, trying to get the shuttle within 1' of the baseline. Usually both *A* and *B* hit to one particular corner until some degree of accuracy is attained, and then the spot is shifted. After both players achieve success in overhand dropping (forehand and backhand) and underhand clearing (forehand and backhand), then you can increase the difficulty of this drill by having *A* drop to either side and by having *B* underhand clear to either side. Both players should return to their center position to make the drill more realistic and closely related to a game situation. (Player who makes the underhand clear can practice footwork with this drill at the same time.)

Figure 8.1 Drills: *A*. The overhead clear. *B*. The overhead drop shot and underhand clear. *C*. The straight drive.

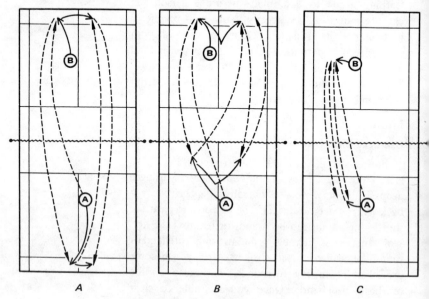

A   B   C

Straight Drive Drill

Both players (*A* and *B*), as illustrated in Fig. 8.1C, start in the center position. *A* starts off with a predetermined drive serve to *B*'s forehand or backhand. *B* should drive the shuttle flat and straight down the side. If *A* hits to *B*'s forehand, and *B* hits a straight drive, this will be followed by a backhand drive by *A*. *Keep the shuttle straight* until the shuttle can be hit repeatedly with direction and control. Cross-courts will be discussed later.

Serving Drill

This drill can be utilized with a partner or by oneself. (See Fig. 8.2A.) Try to use at least ten shuttles when you practice this skill so a definite rhythm and consistency of stroke can be perfected. If working with a partner, the receiver should always let the shuttle drop so the server can see how deep in the court the shuttle is landing. Work on getting it to land between the two lines at the back of the court. Later you will try for a smaller area than this, but get your serve consistently into this area first.

Figure 8.2 Drills and games: *A*. The serving drill. *B*. The short (or net) game.

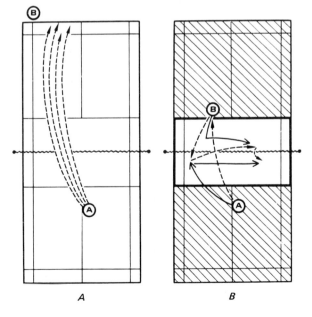

A

B

Short (or Net) Game

This game is played between the two short service lines, with the exception of the initial serve. (See. Fig. 8.2B.) The initial serve must be a normal low doubles service into the proper court. Score exactly like singles and play a regular game. The sideline can be either the singles or doubles lines. This game has value not only in teaching scoring but also in developing your touch on straight and cross-court shots. Any shot which goes past the short service line is out of court and loses the rally.

Smash and Drop (Block) Drill

This drill is valuable for teaching the smash and defense against a smash. (See Fig. 8.3A.) Player *A* serves high to about ¾ court. *B* hits a predetermined straight or cross smash which *A* blocks back over the net. By using 20 or so shuttles, more practice can be accomplished in a short period of time.

Figure 8.3 Drills: *A*. The smash and drop (block). *B*. The overhand clear and drop combination.

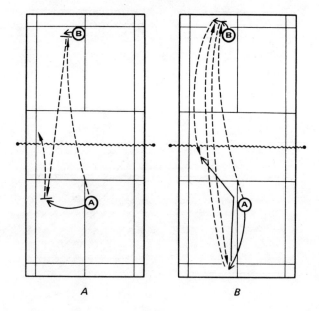

A   *B*

Overhand Clear and Drop Combination Drill

This drill is valuable in teaching the player to use the preliminary windup for both the overhand clear and drop shots. (See Fig. 8.3B.) Player *A* will serve high and deep to player *B*, who hits a deep clear followed by a drop shot. Player *A* will return all of *B*'s shots with a high clear as *B* alternates hitting a clear, drop, clear, drop. After several minutes of this, players change positions and player *A* does the clearing and dropping.

ADVANCED

Half Court Singles Game

This game is valuable in teaching the player to run his opponent up and back in the court. (See Fig. 8.4A.) The court is divided down the middle by an imaginary line which continues the middle line all the way across the court. Play a regular game and keep score. The only difference is that you would serve straight ahead and not diagonally, as must be done in a proper game. A certain amount of control is necessary before the players can utilize this game efficiently.

Figure 8.4 Drills and games: *A.* The half-court singles game. *B.* The smash-drop-clear drill. *C.* The long and short game.

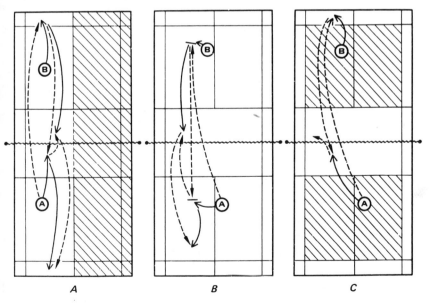

| A | B | C |

Smash-Drop-Clear Drill

This drill is good for working on three skills at one time. (See Fig. 8.4B.) For this reason it is beyond the basic drills and included in the advanced. Player *A* serves high to ¾ court area for *B* to smash. *A* returns *B*'s smash with a drop which *B* clears and *A* smashes. The drill is continued in this manner, with the shuttle being smashed-dropped-cleared by both players until one player makes an error. The position of the smash can be predetermined at first until both players develop the ability to return each other's smash.

Long and Short Game

This game is played and scored like regular singles, except control of the shots is stressed. (See Fig. 8.4C.) Every clear must be hit within the two lines at the back of the court, and all drops must be hit inside the short service line and the net. Any clear or drop not landing in their respective areas are not hit back over the net. This forces each player to concentrate on hitting *deep* clears and *short* drops and avoid playing his strokes into the center of his opponent's court.

Singles Court vs. Baseline Game

This is a very good game to use if the two players are not equal in playing ability. (See. Fig. 8.5A.) The good player *A* is allowed to hit *only* within the last 2½' of the court (between doubles service line and baseline), while the weak player *B* can hit anywhere within the singles court. No matter what shot is hit, *A* must hit the shuttle deep to the back of *B*'s court. The only exception is if *B* hits such a weak return that it would usually be smashed by an opponent. If this happens, *A* can smash but must hit his smash within 1' of either sideline. Regular score is kept.

Alternating Drop-Clear Drill

This is a very good drill for learning to hit on the move and also for conditioning. (See Fig. 8.5B.) It can also be used to give a good player a good workout against a weaker player. If player *A* is to be the runner, he will hit nothing but drop shots to either side of the court. Player *B* will alternate hitting a drop followed by hitting an underhand clear. (Example: *B* serves deep—*A* overhand drops—*B* redrops—*A* redrops—*B* clears—*A* overhand drops—*B* redrops—*A* redrops—*B* clears.) If you can follow this example, you will find that *A* does all the running by dropping from deep followed by running to the net and redropping and then back to the baseline for another overhand drop. *B*, on the other hand, stands at the net and drops to pull *A* into the net; he follows this with an underhand clear to push *A* deep in his court.

Uneven Partners Game

This is a very good game to use when two players are uneven in skill. (See Fig. 8.5C.) Strong player *A* picks out one of the four corners of the court to which he must hit *all* his strokes in the rally. Weak player *B* may hit to any spot on the court he chooses. This is great for helping *A* to develop conditioning and also the ability to hit any shuttle to a specific spot on the court. Player *B* gets the opportunity to use all his strokes without moving excessively and thus practices his control. This can be scored like a regular game or just used as a drill.

Figure 8.5 Drills and games: *A.* The singles court versus the baseline game. *B.* Alternating drop-clear drill. *C.* The uneven partner's game.

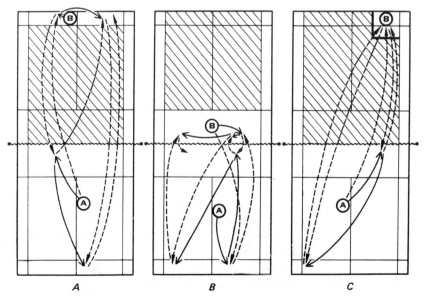

A   B   C

Conditioning

This chapter is mainly for those players who want to compete in tournament play. Several of the previous chapters have been devoted to developing badminton strokes and learning strategy. You must also train to become physically fit if you expect to become a top player, since strokes are useless without the conditioning that must also be developed. There are two types of conditioning that will be discussed in this chapter: (1) general conditioning for overall fitness, and (2) specific conditioning for badminton.

GENERAL CONDITIONING

One of the best methods of developing overall conditioning for any sport is *running*. Little equipment is required and there are always open areas such as school tracks, fields, and streets on which to run. If you are completely out of condition, start slowly and jog only one lap (or two minutes) the first time out. Slowly increase your distance until you can run two miles in 12-14 minutes. Most men will be close to 12 minutes while women will usually be closer to 14 minutes. When you can run two or more miles and recover in a few minutes without excessive discomfort, your general conditioning is good and distance running should be used just for maintaining your overall condition. You are now ready to progress to specific conditioning for badminton.

SPECIFIC CONDITIONING FOR BADMINTON

Players get tired in badminton from quick starts, stops, and changes of direction. Specific conditioning, then, should consist mainly of quick bursts of speed and many changes of direction. Use as many gamelike drills as possible.

Below are a few drills to give the idea of what movements can be stressed.

Alternate Foot Touch. Stand on singles and doubles sideline (facing the court) with one foot on the singles and the other on the doubles sideline. Alternate feet on each line by jumping and exchanging feet as rapidly as possible. How many can you do in 30 seconds? In one minute? Increase this drill until you can do it for five minutes.

Click Feet Together. Stand on the deep doubles service line and the baseline with one foot on each line. Jump and click feet together once and then return feet to the same lines. How many can you do in 30 seconds? In one minute? Increase this drill until you can do it for five minutes.

Shuttle Pickup. Place one shuttle on each of the doubles sidelines. Starting with a shuttle in your hand, run alternately to each side of the court and exchange the shuttle in your hand with the one on the floor. How many can you do in one minute? In five minutes?

Line Touch. On a badminton court (without a net), start at one baseline and run to the short service line, touch the line with one hand and return to the baseline; next, run to the short service line on the opposite side of the court, touch line and return to the baseline; next, run to opposite baseline, touch and return; then run to opposite short service line and to baseline. How long does it take you to do this entire run? Try to shorten your time as much as possible on future runs.

Sprints. (On a track or in a gymnasium) Run forward or backward for twenty yards. Then walk for twenty yards and repeat. Try to accelerate as quickly as possible. Do several of these sprints until you get tired. Increase the number of sprints every day.

Shadow Badminton. Stand in the middle of a badminton court and run to all corners of the court playing an imaginary rally (hit clears, drops and smashes). Return to the center of the court after each imaginary stroke. Work on good footwork during this drill as you tend to do what you practice.

Make your drill more difficult by having a friend stand in the middle of the net and point to different corners. This makes the drill more realistic as you do not know the location of your next move, just as you do not know the location of your opponent's next shot in an actual game.

There are other drills that could be used which are just as good as the ones presented. These are a few that I have seen used effectively in the development of tournament players of championship caliber. Stress the following items when developing conditioning drills: (1) keep them as gamelike as possible; and (2) work on quick starts, stops, and changes of direction as these factors cause you to tire when playing an opponent of equal or better skill.

Accomplishments

Who are the top American players today and throughout the past several years? The top international players? What countries win the Thomas Cup? The Uber Cup? These above questions are continually being asked the author by beginning players and interested people. This chapter is devoted to answering these questions by listing the best players in this country since World War II, the winners of the All England Championships, and the Thomas and Uber Cup International Team Champions. The winners of the All England are usually considered to be the unofficial world champions by most badminton authorities.

As was mentioned previously in the chapter on history, the United States has had two truly outstanding world champions: Dave Freeman and Judy Devlin Hashman. Dave was undefeated in singles from 1939 through 1953 and also won several men's doubles and mixed doubles championships. Judy won 31 U.S. national titles and 17 All England titles since 1954. Other Americans who have made outstanding records include Joe Alston, who was the U.S. No. 1 in singles on five occasions, 14 straight years U.S. No. 1 in men's doubles with Wynn Rogers, and seven times mixed champion with his wife Lois.

Besides winning 14 doubles titles with Alston, Wynn Rogers won the men's doubles on three other occasions, and the mixed doubles eight times since World War II with five different partners.

Ethel Marshall was U. S. No. 1 in singles for seven straight years after World War II and also won two doubles and three mixed championships.

Jim Poole was U. S. No. 1 in singles for ten straight years (except for two years when Channarong Ratanaseangsuang of Thailand was ranked as an American). Jim has also been No. 1 in men's doubles with Don Paup for eight straight years and mixed doubles champion for two years.

Tyna Barinaga has been U.S. No. 1 on three occasions in singles, six times in ladies doubles and twice in mixed doubles (once with Canadian star player Wayne MacDonnell and once with Jim Poole).

Listed below are the U.S., All England, and International Team Champions.

U. S. NATIONAL RANKINGS (1947–72)

	Men's Singles		Ladies' Singles		Men's Doubles
1947	D. Freeman	1947	E. Marshall	1947	D. Freeman-W. Kimball
1948	D. Freeman	1948	E. Marshall	1948	D. Freeman-W. Rogers
1949	D. Freeman	1949	E. Marshall	1949	W. Rogers-B. McCay
1950	M. Mendez	1950	E. Marshall	1950	W. Rogers-B. McCay
1951	J. Alston	1951	E. Marshall	1951	J. Alston-W. Rogers
1952	M. Mendez	1952	E. Marshall	1952	J. Alston-W. Rogers
1953	D. Freeman	1953	E. Marshall	1953	J. Alston-W. Rogers
1954	J. Alston	1954	M. Varner	1954	J. Alston-W. Rogers
1955	J. Alston	1955	J. Devlin	1955	J. Alston-W. Rogers
1956	J. Alston	1956	J. Devlin	1956	J. Alston-W. Rogers
1957	J. Alston	1957	J. Devlin	1957	J. Alston-W. Rogers
1958	R. Palmer	1958	J. Devlin	1958	J. Alston-W. Rogers
1959	J. Poole	1959	J. Devlin	1959	J. Alston-W. Rogers
1960	J. Poole	1960	J. Devlin	1960	J. Alston-W. Rogers
1961	J. Poole	1961	J. Devlin Hashman	1961	J. Alston-W. Rogers
1962	J. Poole	1962	J. Devlin Hashman	1962	J. Alston-W. Rogers
1963	J. Poole	1963	J. Devlin Hashman	1963	J. Alston-W. Rogers
1964	C. Ratanaseangsuang	1964	D. O'Neil	1964	J. Alston-W. Rogers
1965	C. Ratanaseangsuang	1965	J. Devlin Hashman	1965	J. Poole-D. Paup
1966	J. Poole	1966	J. Devlin Hashman	1966	J. Poole-D. Paup
1967	J. Poole	1967	J. Devlin Hashman	1967	J. Poole-D. Paup
1968	J. Poole	1968	T. Barinaga	1968	J. Poole-D. Paup
1969	S. Hales	1969	T. Barinaga	1969	J. Poole-D. Paup
1970	R. Starkey	1970	T. Barinaga	1970	J. Poole-D. Paup
1971	R. Starkey/S. Hales	1971	D. Hales	1971	J. Poole-D. Paup
1972	C. Kinard	1972	P. Stockton	1972	J. Poole-D. Paup

Ladies' Doubles

1947	J. Wright-T. Scovil
1948	J. Wright-T. Scovil
1949	J. Wright-T. Scovil
1950	J. Wright-T. Scovil
1951	D. Hann-L. Smith
1952	E. Marshall-B. Massman
1953	J. Devlin-S. Devlin
1954	J. Devlin-S. Devlin
1955	J. Devlin-S. Devlin
1956	E. Marshall-B. Massman
1957	J. Devlin-S. Devlin
1958	J. Devlin-S. Devlin
1959	J. Devlin-S. Devlin
1960	J. Devlin-S. Devlin
1961	J. Devlin Hashman-S. Devlin Peard
1962	J. Devlin Hashman-P. Stephens
1963	L. Alston-D. Haase
1964	T. Barinaga-C. Jensen
1965	T. Barinaga-C. Jensen
1966	T. Barinaga-C. Jensen
1967	J. Devlin Hashman-R. Junes
1968	T. Barinaga-H. Tibbetts
1969	T. Barinaga-H. Tibbetts
1970	T. Barinaga-C. Jensen Hein
1971	C. Jensen Hein-C. Starkey
1972	P. Stockton-P. Bretzke

Mixed Doubles

1947	W. Rogers-V. Hill
1948	C. Stephens-P. Stephens
1949	W. Rogers-L. Smith
1950	W. Rogers-L. Smith
1951	W. Rogers-L. Smith
1952	W. Rogers-H. Tibbetts
1953	J. Alston-L. Alston
1954	W. Rogers-D. Hann
1955	J. Alston-L. Alston
1956	B. Williams-E. Marshall
1957	B. Williams-E. Marshall
1958	B. Williams-E. Marshall
1959	M. Roche-J. Devlin
1960	M. Roche-J. Devlin
1961	W. Rogers-J. Devlin Hashman
1962	W. Rogers-J. Devlin Hashman
1963	J. Alston-L. Alston
1964	J. Alston-L. Alston
1965	J. Alston-L. Alston
1966	J. Alston-L. Alston
1967	J. Alston-L. Alston
1968	L. Saben-C. Starkey
1969	D. Paup-H. Tibbetts
1970	J. Poole-T. Barinaga
1971	J. Poole-M. Breckell/D. Paup-H. Tibbetts
1972	T. Carmichael-P. Stockton

ALL-ENGLAND CHAMPIONSHIPS (1947-72)

Men's Singles

1947	C. Jepsen (Sweden)
1948	J. Skaarup (Denmark)
1949	D. Freeman (U.S.A.)
1950	Wong Pen Soon (Malaya)
1951	Wong Pen Soon (Malaya)
1952	Wong Pen Soon (Malaya)
1953	E. Choong (Malaya)
1954	E. Choong (Malaya)
1955	Wong Pen Soon (Malaya)
1956	E. Choong (Malaya)
1957	E. Choong (Malaya)
1958	E. Kops (Denmark)
1959	Tan Joe Hok (Indonesia)
1960	E. Kops (Denmark)
1961	E. Kops (Denmark)
1962	E. Kops (Denmark)
1963	E. Kops (Denmark)
1964	K. Nielson (Denmark)
1965	E. Kops (Denmark)
1966	Tan Aik Huang (Malaysia)

Men's Doubles

1947	T. Madsen & P. Holm (Denmark)
1948	P. Dabelsteen & B. Frederiksen (Denmark)
1949	Ooi Teik Hock & Teoh Seng Khoon (Malaya)
1950	P. Dabelsteen & J. Skaarup (Denmark)
1951	E. Choong & E. B. Choong (Malaya)
1952	E. L. Choong & E. B. Choong (Malaya)
1953	E. L. Choong & E. B. Choong (Malaya)
1954	Ooi Teik Hock & Ong Poh Lim (Malaya)
1955	F. Kobbero & J. Hansen (Denmark)
1956	F. Kobbero & J. Hansen (Denmark)
1957	J. Alston (U.S.A.) & H. Heah (Malaya)
1958	E. Kops & E. Nielsen (Denmark)
1959	Lim Say Hup & Teh Kew San (Malaya)
1960	F. Kobbero & E. Nielsen (Denmark)
1961	F. Kobbero & J. Hansen (Denmark)
1962	F. Kobbero & J. Hansen (Denmark)
1963	F. Kobbero & J. Hansen (Denmark)
1964	F. Kobbero & J. Hansen (Denmark)
1965	Ng Boon Bee & Tan Yee Kahn (Malaysia)
1966	Ng Boon Bee & Tan Kee Kahn (Malaysia)

ALL-ENGLAND CHAMPIONSHIPS (Cont.)

Men's Singles

1967   E. Kops (Denmark)
1968   R. Hartono (Indonesia)
1969   R. Hartono (Indonesia)
1970   R. Hartono (Indonesia)
1971   R. Hartono (Indonesia)
1972   R. Hartono (Indonesia)

Men's Doubles

1967   H. Borch & E. Kops (Denmark)
1968   H. Borch & E. Kops (Denmark)
1969   H. Borch & E. Kops (Denmark)
1970   T. Bacher & P. Petersen (Denmark)
1971   Ng Boon Bee & P. Gunalan (Malaysia)
1972   Christian & Ade Chandra (Indonesia)

Ladies' Singles

1947   M. Ussing (Denmark)
1948   K. Thorndahl (Denmark)
1949   A. Schiott Jacobsen (Denmark)
1950   T. Ahm (Denmark)
1951   A. Jacobsen (Denmark)
1952   T. Ahm (Denmark)
1953   M. Ussing (Denmark)
1954   J. Devlin (U.S.A.)
1955   M. Varner (U.S.A.)
1956   M. Varner (U.S.A.)
1957   J. Devlin (U.S.A.)
1958   J. Devlin (U.S.A.)
1959   H. M. Ward (England)
1960   J. Devlin (U.S.A.)
1961   J. Devlin Hashman (U.S.A.)
1962   J. Devlin Hashman (U.S.A.)

1963   J. Devlin Hashman (U.S.A.)
1964   J. Devlin Hashman (U.S.A.)
1965   U. Smith (England)
1966   J. Devlin Hashman (U.S.A.)
1967   J. Devlin Hashman (U.S.A.)
1968   E. Twedberg (Sweden)

1969   H. Yuki (Japan)
1970   E. Takenaka (Japan)
1971   E. Twedberg (Sweden)
1972   N. Takagi (Japan)

Ladies' Doubles

1947   K. Thorndahl & T. Olsen (Denmark)
1948   K. Thorndahl & G. Ahm (Denmark)
1949   H. Uber & Q. Allen (England)
1950   K. Thorndahl & G. Ahm (Denmark)
1951   K. Thorndahl & G. Ahm (Denmark)
1952   A. Jacobsen & G. Ahm (Denmark)
1953   I. Cooley & J. White (England)
1954   S. Devlin & J. Devlin (U.S.A.)
1955   I. Cooley & J. White (England)
1956   S. Devlin & J. Devlin (U.S.A.)
1957   A. Hansen & K. Granlund (Denmark)
1958   M. Varner & H. Ward (U.S.A. & England)
1959   W. Rogers & E. Timperley (England)
1960   S. Devlin & J. Devlin (U.S.A.)
1961   G. Hashman & F. Peard (U.S.A. & Ireland)
1962   G. Hashman & T. Holst-Christensen
　　　　　(U.S.A. & Denmark)
1963   G. Hashman & F. Peard (U.S.A. & Ireland)
1964   K. Jorgensen & U. Rasmussen (Denmark)
1965   K. Jorgensen & U. Strand (Denmark)
1966   G. Hashman & F. Peard (U.S.A. & Ireland)
1967   I. Rietveld & U. Strand
　　　　　(Netherlands & Denmark)
1968   Minarni & R. Koestijah (Indonesia)
1969   M. Boxall & P. Whetnall (England)
1970   M. Boxall & P. Whetnall (England)
1971   N. Takagi & H. Yuki (Japan)
1972   N. Takagi & H. Yuki (Japan)

Mixed Doubles

1947   P. Holm & T. Olsen (Denmark)
1948   J. Skaarup & K. Thorndahl (Denmark)
1949   C. Stephens & P. Stephens (U.S.A.)
1950   P. Holm & G. Ahm (Denmark)
1951   P. Holm & G. Ahm (Denmark)
1952   P. Holm & G. Ahm (Denmark)
1953   E. Choong & J. White (Malaya & England)
1954   J. Best & I. Cooley (England)
1955   F. Kobbero & K. Thorndahl (Denmark)
1956   A. D. Jordan & E. Timperley (England)
1957   F. Kobbero & K. Granlund (Denmark)
1958   A. D. Jordan & E. Timperley (England)
1959   P. Nielsen & I. Hansen (Denmark)

ALL-ENGLAND CHAMPIONSHIPS (Cont.)

Mixed Doubles

1960 F. Kobbero & K. Granlund (Denmark)
1961 F. Kobbero & K. Granlund (Denmark)
1962 F. Kobbero & U. Rasmussen (Denmark)
1963 F. Kobbero & U. Rasmussen (Denmark)
1964 A. D. Jordan & J. Pritchard (England)
1965 F. Kobbero & U. Strand (Denmark)
1966 F. Kobbero & U. Strand (Denmark)
1967 S. Andersen & U. Strand (Denmark)
1968 A. D. Jordan & S. Pound (England)
1969 R. Mills & G. Perrin (England)
1970 P. Walsoe & P. Hansen (Denmark)
1971 S. Pri & U. Strand (Denmark)
1972 S. Pri & U. Strand (Denmark)

THOMAS CUP CHAMPIONS (MEN)

The Thomas Cup was donated by Sir George Thomas and international team competition for men was started in 1948 and is held every three years.

Contests	Champion Nation	Runner-up
1948-49	Malaya	Denmark
1951-52	Malaya	U.S.A.
1954-55	Malaya	Denmark
1957-58	Indonesia	Malaya
1960-61	Indonesia	Thailand
1963-64	Indonesia	Denmark
1966-67	Malaysia	Indonesia
1969-70	Indonesia	Malaysia

UBER CUP CHAMPIONS (WOMEN)

The Uber Cup was donated by Mrs. H. S. Uber and international team competition for women was started in 1956 and is held every three years.

Contests	Champion Nation	Runner-up
1956-57	U.S.A.	Denmark
1959-60	U.S.A.	Denmark
1962-63	U.S.A.	England
1965-66	Japan	U.S.A.
1968-69	Japan	Indonesia
1971-72	Japan	Indonesia

As can be seen by the above results, the U.S.A. has not won the Thomas Cup but did win the Uber Cup on three occasions. The Far East countries of Japan, Indonesia, and Malaysia have dominated the Thomas Cup and Uber Cup results since 1963. It is also interesting to note that badminton is the national sport of these countries along with soccer.

Terminology

ABA American Badminton Association, national governing body in the United States, founded in 1936.

ALLEY The 1½' extension on both sides of the court used in doubles play.

ATTACKING CLEAR A shot hit to barely clear the racket of your opponent and carry to the back of his court. Sometimes called an offensive clear.

BACK ALLEY Area between the back boundary line and the long service line in doubles. This area is 2½' in depth.

BACKCOURT The back half of the court in the general area of the back boundary lines.

BACKHAND The nonracket side of the body. For right-handed players is would be on the left side of the body and includes all strokes made on this side.

BASELINE The lines parallel to the net which limit the playing area at the end boundaries of the court.

BASE The spot approximately in the center of the court to which a player tries to return after each shot.

BIRD   A commonly used term for the shuttle, the missile used in place of a ball.

BLOCK   Placing the racket in front of the shuttle and letting it rebound off the racket to the opponent's side of the court. Very little stroke is made.

CARRY   Holding the shuttle on the racket during the execution of a stroke. This is an illegal shot. Usually the shuttle will leave the racket in a direction different than the player intended to hit it.

CLEAR (OR LOB)   A high, deep shot hit to the back of the opponent's court.

COMBINATION DOUBLES FORMATION   A combination of the side-by-side and the up-and-back formations. Explained more fully in Chapter 8.

COURT   Area of play. Although the size varied during the 1800s, it has been standardized since the 1930's. It is 20' by 44' for doubles and 17' by 44' for singles.

CROSS-COURT   A stroke hit diagonally from one side of the court to the other.

DECEPTION   Deceiving one's opponent by changing the direction and speed of the shuttle at the last second.

DOUBLE HIT   Hitting the shuttle twice in succession on the same stroke. This is illegal.

DRIVE   A hard, flat shot which makes a horizontal flight across the net. Usually hit close to the net as it crosses and downward when possible.

DRIVE SERVE   A hard, quick serve with a flat trajectory. Usually used in doubles and aimed at the opponent's head or left shoulder.

DROP   A stroke which just clears the net and immediately starts to fall in the opponent's court.

FAULT   A violation of the rules. Faults can be during service, by both server or receiver, or during play.

FIRST SERVICE   A term used in doubles to indicate that the team still has both its serves.

FLICK SERVE   Used in doubles when your opponent is expecting a low serve. A quick wrist and forearm rotation changes a soft shot into a faster passing shot.

FOOT FAULT   A violation of the rules in which the feet of the server, or receiver, are not in the position required by the laws. This could be illegal position and/or movement.

FORECOURT   This is the area of the court nearest the net; usually refers to the area between the net and the short service line.

FOREHAND   The racket side of the body. For right-handed players it would be the right side of the body and includes all strokes made on this side.

GAME   The unit of points necessary to win the game. Fifteen points in men's singles and in all doubles constitute a game; eleven points constitute a game in ladies' singles. (See *Setting*.)

GAME BIRD   The point that will enable the server to win the game.

HAIRPIN NET SHOT   Stroke made from below and close to the net with the shuttle rising and just clearing the net to fall sharply downward on the opposite side. Name is taken from the path of the shuttle's flight.

HALF-COURT SHOT   A shot played to midcourt, usually low, used in doubles and mixed doubles against up-and-back formations.

HAND-IN   Term used to show that the player serving still retains the service.

HAND-OUT   Term used to show that one player in doubles has lost his service.

IBF   International Badminton Federation, the world governing body founded in 1934.

INNING   The terms of service. Time during which a player or team holds the service.

KILL   A fast, downward return which usually cannot be returned.

LET   A legitimate stoppage of play due to interference from outside the court. It can also be called after a rally if a player or team served to received in the wrong court (depending on who wins the rally). It is replayed. (Refer to Laws 12 and 17.)

LOVE   A term used to indicate no score. If the score is "3–love," it means the server has three and his opponent has zero. Umpire usually starts singles games by calling "love–all, play."

LOVE–ALL   A term which indicates the score is 0–0. I is also used when a game has been set. (See *Setting*.)

MATCH   A match is usually best two out of three games.

MATCH POINT   The point which, if won by the server, wins the match.

MIDCOURT   The center of the court area approximately halfway between the net and the back boundary line.

NET SHOT   A shot played in the forecourt that barely clears the net and then drops rapidly.

OBSTRUCTION   When a player hinders an opponent from playing the shot. Usually called if a player who hits a poor net shot holds his racket up at the net and disconcerts his opponent, who is trying to kill this poor shot.

OVERHEAD   A stroke played above head height.

PASSING SHOT   A shot that goes past an opponent to the side, as constrasted to one going over his head.

RACKET (OR RACQUET)   The implement used in the hand to hit the shuttle.

RALLY   The exchange of strokes back and forth while the shuttle is in play until it becomes dead.

READY POSITION   The alert position that the player assumes just before the opponent strokes the shuttle. It is usually with slightly flexed knees and racket held about chest high.

RECEIVER   The player who receives the service.

ROUND-THE-HEAD-SHOT   A forehand stroke made on the backhand side of the body. Usually hit overhead and can be either a clear, drop, or smash.

RUSH THE SERVE   Quick move to the net by the receiver after the serve has been struck to put away a low serve that is weak. Used mostly in doubles and mixed doubles play.

SECOND SERVICE   A term used in doubles play to indicate that one person has lost his service and is "down"; his partner still retains his serve.

SERVE OR SERVICE   The act of putting the shuttle into play by hitting it into the opponent's court.

SERVER   The player who delivers the service.

SERVICE COURT   The area into which the serve must be delivered. This area will depend on whether it is singles or doubles, and also depends on the score.

SETTING   The method of extending the game by playing additional points when the score is tied at specific scores in a game. The player or team reaching this score first has the option of setting.

SHORT SERVICE LINE   The line 6½' from the net that serves must cross to be legal.

SHUTTLECOCK   The official name for the shuttle or bird. The shuttles today are of two types: (1) goose feathers, and (2) nylon.

SIDE IN   This term refers to the side whose turn it is to serve.

SIDE OUT   This occurs when the side that is serving loses the serve and becomes the receiving team.

SIDE-BY-SIDE FORMATION   A doubles formation used in either regular doubles or mixed doubles.

SLING OR THROW   The term to indicate that the shuttle was carried by the racket. It is illegal.

SMASH   The hard overhead stroke hit downward with great force. It is the principal attacking stroke in badminton.

STROKE   The action of striking the shuttle with the racket.

UNDERHAND   A stroke which is made when the shuttle is contacted below the level of the shoulders. It usually refers to a shot being hit upward.

UNSIGHT   When the partner of the server stands in such a position that the receiver cannot see the serve being struck. This is illegal.

UP-AND-BACK FORMATION   A doubles and mixed doubles formation. The predominant formation that is used in mixed.

WOOD SHOT   The shot which results when the shuttle is struck by the frame of the racket. A legal shot under the present rules.

The Laws of Badminton

RULES[1]

Court

1. (a) The court shall be laid out as shown in Fig.1.2.1A (except in the case provided for in paragraph (b) of this Law) and to the measurements there shown, and shall be defined by white, black or other easily distinguishable lines, 1½" wide.

    In marking the court, the width (1½") of the center lines shall be equally divided between the right and left service courts; the width (1½" each) of the short service line and the long service line shall fall within the 13' measurement given as the length of the service court; and the width (1½" each) of all other boundary lines shall fall within the measurements given.

    (b) Where space does not permit the marking out of a court for doubles, a court may be marked out for singles only as shown in Fig. 12.1B. The back boundary lines become also the long service

[1] As adopted by the International Badminton Federation, incorporating all amendments subsequently adopted. Reprinted with their permission.

lines, and the posts, or the strips of materials representing them as referred to in Law 2, shall be placed on the side lines.

Posts

2. The posts shall be 5'–1'' in height from the floor. They shall be sufficiently firm to keep the net strained as provided in Law 3, and shall be placed on the side boundary lines of the court.

Figure 12.1 The badminton court.

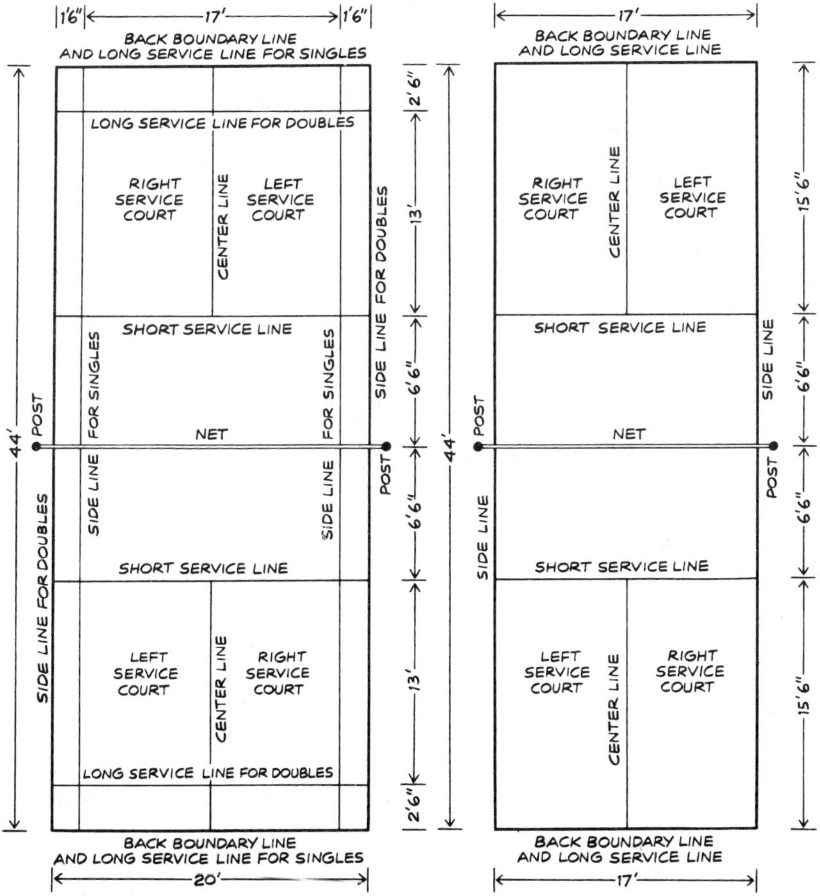

A. Doubles court.

B. Singles court.

Where this is not practicable, some method must be employed for indicating the position of the side boundary line where it passes under the net, e.g., by the use of a thin post or strip of material, not less than 1½" in width, fixed to the side boundary line and rising vertically to the net cord. Where this is in use on a court marked for doubles it shall be placed on the side boundary line of the doubles court irrespective of whether singles or doubles are being played.

Net

3. The net shall be made of fine tanned cord of from 5/8" to 3/4" mesh. It shall be firmly stretched from post to post, and shall be 2'–6" in depth. The top of the net shall be 5' in height from the floor at the center, and 5'–1" at the posts, and shall be edged with a 3" white tape doubled and supported by a cord or cable run through the tape and strained over and flush with the top of the posts.

Shuttle

4. A shuttle shall weigh from 73 to 85 grains and shall have from 14 to 16 feathers fixed in a cork, 1" to 1 1/8" in diameter. The feathers shall be from 2½" to 2¾" in length from the tip to the top of the cork base. They shall have from 2 1/8" to 2½" spread at the top and shall be firmly fastened with thread or other suitable material.

Subject to there being no substantial variation in the general design, pace, weight, and flight of the shuttle, modifications in the above specifications may be made, subject to the approval of the National Organizations concerned:

(a) in places where atmospheric conditions, due either to altitude or climate, made the standard shuttle unsuitable; or

(b) if special circumstances exist which make it otherwise expedient in the interest of the game.

A shuttle shall be deemed to be of correct pace if, when a player of average strength strikes it with a full underhand stroke from a spot immediately above one back boundary line in a line parallel to the side lines, and at an upward angle, it falls not less than 1' and not more than 2'–6" short of the other back boundary line.

Players

5. (a) The word "Player" applies to all those taking part in a game.

(b) The game shall be played, in the case of the doubles game, by two players a side, and in the case of the singles game, by one player a side.

(c) The side for the time being having the right to serve shall be called the "In" side, and the opposing side shall be called the "Out" side.

Toss

6. Before commencing play the opposing sides shall toss, and the side winning the toss shall have the option of:

(a) Serving first; or

(b) Not serving first; or

(c) Choosing ends.

The side losing the toss shall then have the choice of any alternative remaining.

Scoring

7. (a) The doubles and men's singles game consists of 15 or 21 points, as may be arranged. Provided that in a game of 15 points, when the score is 13 all, the side which first reached 13 has the option of "setting" the game to 5, and that when the score is 14 all, the side which first reached 14 has the option of "setting" the game to 3. After a game has been "set" the score is called "love all," and the side which first scores 5 to 3 points, according as the game has been "set" at 13 all or 14 all, wins the game. In either case the claim to "set" the game must be made before the next service is delivered after

the score has reached 13 all or 14 all. Provided also that in a game of 21 points the same method of scoring be adopted, substituting 19 and 20 for 13 and 14.

(b) The ladies' singles game consists of 11 points. Provided that when the score is "9 all" the player who first reached 9 has the option of "setting" the game to 3, and when the score is "10 all" the player who first reached 10 has the option of "setting" the game to 2.

(c) A side rejecting the option of "setting" at the first opportunity shall not thereby be debarred from "setting" if a second opportunity arises.

(d) In handicap games "setting" is not permitted.

8. The opposing sides shall contest the best of three games, unless otherwise agreed. The players shall change ends at the commencement of the second game and also of the third game (if any). In the third game the players shall change ends when the leading score reaches:

(a) 8 in a game of 15 points;

(b) 6 in a game of 11 points;

(c) 11 in a game of 21 points;

or, in handicap events, when one of the sides has scored half the total number of points required to win the game (the next highest number being taken in case of fractions). When it has been agreed to play only one game the players shall change ends as provided above for the third game.

If, inadvertently, the players omit to change ends as provided in this Law at the score indicated, the ends shall be changed immediately the mistake is discovered, and the existing score shall stand.

Doubles Play

9. (a) It having been decided which side is to have the first service, the player in the right-hand service court of that side commences the game by serving to the player in the service court diagonally opposite. If the latter player returns the shuttle before it touches the ground, it is to

be returned by one of the "In" side, and then returned by one of the "Out" side, and so on, till a fault is made or the shuttle ceases to be "in play" (vide paragraph (b)). If a fault is made by the "In" side its right to continue serving is lost, as only one player on the side beginning a game is entitled to do so (vide Law 11), and the opponent in the right-hand service court then becomes the server; but if the service is not returned, or the fault is made by the "Out" side, the "In" side scores a point. The "In" side players then change from one service court to the other, the service now being from the left-hand service court to the player in the service court diagonally opposite. So long as a side remains "in," service is delivered alternately from each service court into the one diagonally opposite, the change being made by the "In" side when, and only when, a point is added to its score.

(b) The first service of a side in each inning shall be made from the right-hand service court. A "Service" is delivered as soon as the shuttle is struck by the server's racket. The shuttle is thereafter "in play" until it touches the ground, or until a fault or "let" occurs, or except as provided in Law 19. After the service is delivered the server and the player served to may take up any position they choose on their side of the net, irrespective of any boundary lines.

10. The player served to may alone receive the service, but should the shuttle touch, or be struck by, his partner the "In" side scores a point. No player may receive two consecutive services in the same game, except as provided in Law 12.

11. Only one player of the side beginning a game shall be entitled to serve in its first inning. In all subsequent innings each partner shall have the right, and they shall serve consecutively. The side winning a game shall always serve first in the next game, but either of the winners may serve and either of the losers may receive the service.

12. If a player serves out of turn, or from the wrong service court (owing to a mistake as to the service court from which service is at the time being in order), *and his side wins the rally*, it

shall be a "Let," provided that such "Let" be claimed or allowed before the next succeeding service is delivered.

If a player standing in the wrong service court takes the service, *and his side wins the rally*, it shall be a "Let," provided that such "Let" be claimed or allowed before the next succeeding service is delivered.

If in either of the above cases the side at fault *loses the rally*, the mistake shall stand and the player's positions shall not be corrected during the remainder of the game.

Should a player inadvertently change sides when he should not do so, and the mistake not be discovered until after the next succeeding service has been delivered, the mistake shall stand, and a "Let" cannot be claimed or allowed, and the player's position shall not be corrected during the remainder of that game.

Singles Play

13. In singles Laws 9 to 12 hold good except that:

    (a) The players shall serve from and receive in their respective right-hand service courts only when the server's score is 0 or an even number of points in the game, the service being delivered from and received in their respective left-hand service courts when the server's score is an odd number of points.

    (b) Both players shall change service courts after each point has been scored.

Faults

14. A fault made by a player of the side which is "In," puts the server out; if made by a player whose side is "Out," it counts a point to the "In" side.

    It is a fault:

    (a) If in service, the shuttle at the instant of being struck be higher than the server's waist, or if any part of the head of the racket, at the instant of striking the shuttle, be higher than any part of the server's hand holding the racket.

(b)   If, in serving, the shuttle falls into the wrong service court (i.e., into the one not diagonally opposite the server), or falls short of the short service line or beyond the long service line, or outside the side boundary lines of the service court into which service is in order.

(c)   If the server's feet are not in the service court from which service is at the time being in order, or if the feet of the player receiving the service are not in the service court diagonally opposite until the service is delivered. (Vide Law 16.)

(d)   If before or during the delivery of the service any player makes preliminary feints or otherwise intentionally balks his opponent.

(e)   If, either in service or play, the shuttle falls outside the boundaries of the court, or passes through or under the net, or fails to pass the net, or touches the roof or side walls, or the person or dress of a player. (A shuttle falling on a line shall be deemed to have fallen in the court or service court of which such line is a boundary.)

(f)   If the shuttle "in play" be struck before it crosses to the striker's side of the net. (The striker may, however, follow the shuttle over the net with his racket in the course of his stroke.)

(g)   If, when the shuttle is "in play," a player touches the net or its supports with racket, person or dress.

(h)   If the shuttle be held on the racket (i.e., caught or slung) during the execution of a stroke; or if the shuttle be hit twice in succession by the same player with two strokes; or if the shuttle be hit by a player and his partner successively.

(i)   If, in play, a player strikes the shuttle (unless he thereby makes a good return) or is struck by it, whether he is standing within or outside the boundaries of the court.

(j)   If a player obstructs an opponent.

(k)   If Law 16 be transgressed.

General

15. The server shall not serve till his opponent is ready, but the opponent shall be deemed to be ready if a return of the service be attempted.

16. The server and the player served to must stand within the limits of their respective service courts (as bounded by the short and long service, the center, and side lines), and some part of both feet of these players must remain in contact with the ground in a stationary position until the service is delivered. A foot on or touching a line in the case of either the server or the receiver shall be held to be outside his service court (vide Law 14 (c)). The respective partners may take up any position, provided they do not unsight or otherwise obstruct an opponent.

17. (a) If, in the course of service or rally, the shuttle touches and passes over the net, the stroke is not invalidated thereby. It is a good return if the shuttle having passed outside either post drops on or within the boundary lines of the opposite court. A "Let" may be given by the umpire for any unforeseen or accidental hindrance.

    (b) If, in service, or during a rally, a shuttle, *after passing over the net*, is caught in or on the net, it is a "Let."

    (c) If the receiver is faulted for moving before the service is delivered, or for not being within the correct service court, in accordance with Laws 14(c) or 16, and at the same time the server is also faulted for a service infringement, it shall be a "Let."

    (d) When a "Let" occurs, the play since the last service shall not count, and the player who served shall serve again except when Law 12 is applicable.

18. If the server, in attempting to serve, misses the shuttle, it is not a fault; but if the shuttle be touched by the racket, a service is thereby delivered.

19. If, when in play, the shuttle strikes the net and remains suspended there, or strikes the net and falls toward the ground on the striker's side of the net, or hits the ground outside the court and an opponent then touches the net or shuttle with his racket or person, there is no penalty, as the shuttle is not *then* in play.

20. If a player has a chance of striking the shuttle in a downward direction when quite near the net, his opponent must not put up his racket near the net on the chance of the shuttle rebounding from it. This is obstruction within the meaning of Law 14(j).

    A player may, however, hold up his racket to protect his face from being hit if he does not thereby balk his opponent.

21. It shall be the duty of the umpire to call "fault" or "Let" should either occur, without appeal being made by the players, and to give his decision on any appeal regarding a point in dispute, if made before the next service; and also to appoint linesmen and service judges at his discretion. The umpire's decision shall be final, but he shall uphold the decision of a linesman or service judge. This shall not preclude the umpire also from faulting the server or receiver. Where, however, a referee is appointed, an appeal shall lie to him from the decision of an umpire on questions of law only.

Continuous Play

22. Play shall be continuous from the first service until the match be concluded; except that (a) in the International Badminton Championship and in the Ladies' International Badminton Championship there shall be allowed an interval not exceeding five minutes between the second and third games of a match; (b) in countries where climate conditions render it desirable, there shall be allowed, subject to the previously published approval of the national organization concerned, an interval not exceeding five minutes between the second and third games of a match, either singles or doubles or both; and (c) when necessitated by circumstances not within the control of the players, the umpire may suspend play for such a period as he may consider necessary. If play be suspended the existing score shall stand and play be resumed from that point. Under no circumstances shall play be suspended to enable a player to recover his strength or wind, or to receive instruction or advice. Except in the case of an interval provided for above, no player shall be allowed to receive advice during a match or to leave the court until the match be concluded without the umpire's consent. The umpire shall be the sole judge of any suspension of play and he shall have the right to disqualify an offender.

INTERPRETATIONS

1. Any movement or conduct by the server that has the effect of breaking the continuity of service after the server and receiver have taken their position to serve and to receive the service is a preliminary feint (Vide Law 14(d)).

2. It is obstruction if a player invade an opponent's court with racket or person in any degree except as permitted in Law 14(f).

3. Where necessary on account of the structure of a building, the local Badminton Authority may, subject to the right of veto of its National Organization, make by-laws dealing with cases in which a shuttle touches an obstruction.

INTERNATIONAL SPECIFICATION FOR THE HEIGHT OF A COURT

This regulation shall apply to all official international matches; to Thomas Cup and Uber Cup; and to all tournaments of the status of a national open championship, or greater, as may be sanctioned by the IBF.

The height of the court for international competitive play shall be a minimum of 26' from the floor over the full court. This height shall be entirely free of girders and other obstructions over the area of the court.

There shall also be at least 4' clear space surrounding all the outer lines of the court, this space being also a minimum requirement between any two courts marked out side by side.

Figure 12.2 Legal and illegal racket head positions.

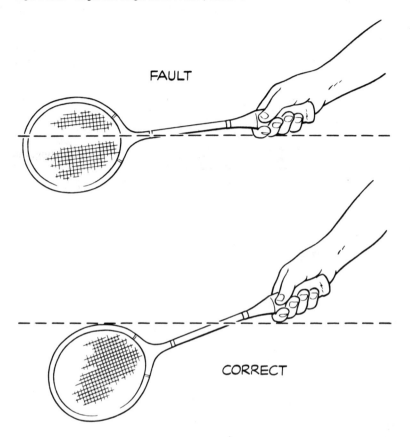

Suggested Readings

BOOKS

Bloss, Margaret Varner. *Badminton,* 2nd edition. Dubuque, Iowa: Wm. C. Brown Co., 1971.

Davidson, Kenneth, and Leland Gustavson. *Winning Badminton.* New York: The Ronald Press Co., 1953.

Davis, Pat *Badminton Complete.* Cranbury, N. J.: A. S. Barnes and Co., 1967.

Hall, J. Tillman et al. *Fundamentals of Physical Education.* Pacific Palisades, Calif.: Goodyear Publishing Co., 1969.

Hashman, Judy Devlin. *Badminton A Champion's Way.* London: Kaye and Ward, 1969.

Rogers, Winn. *Advanced Badminton.* Dubuque, Iowa: Wm. C. Brown Co., 1971.

MAGAZINES AND GUIDES

Badminton Gazette, Official publication of the Badminton Association of England. 81a High Street, Bromley, Kent, England.

Badminton, U.S.A., Official publication of the American Badminton Association. Bea Massman, 333 Saratoga Road, Buffalo, N. Y., 14226.

Ideas for Badminton Instruction, Lifetime Sports Education Project, American Association for Health, Physical Education, and Recreation. 1201 Sixteenth Street, N.W., Washington, D.C., 1966.

International Badminton Federation Handbook, H. A. E. Scheele, 81a High Street, Bromley, Kent, England.

Tennis-Badminton Guide, Division for Girls' and Women's Sports, American Association for Health, Physical Education, and Recreation. 1201 Sixteenth St., N.W., Washington, D.C.

Student/Teacher
Instructional Objectives

Comments on the Use of the Student/Teacher Evaluation Forms

The forms which follow were designed to be used in a variety of instructional settings. Preplanning and organization are necessary for these devices to be used as effectively as possible. The purpose of evaluation is for gauging how well the course objectives are accomplished. That is, evaluation will indicate the progress and the extent to which learning has occurred.

Although the learner *must do his own learning*, the teacher's role is to guide and to direct learning experiences and to provide for appropriate measurement procedures. The charts which follow have been constructed to place primary responsibility on the individual student for estimating progress and indicating areas which need work. It may not be either necessary or desirable to use all the materials provided here in a given teaching learning situation. The instructor and the student should work together to select the materials most appropriate for the course.

It must be remembered that sufficient time for practice and study must be provided if the individual is to perfect his skills as well to accrue knowledge and to develop understanding. The time available may not be adequate for *all* students to demonstrate acceptable levels of skill performance. The instructor may wish to supplement the evaluation devices with a written test covering analysis of performance, procedures, and rules. (Sample tests will be available in a separate instructor's manual covering the entire Goodyear Physical Activities series.) The written test provides an opportunity for the student to demonstrate his knowledge and understanding of the skill even though his actual skill might be less than desired. Final evaluation for grading purposes should take into account a number of variables which may have an influence on individual performance.

STUDENT **SERVES** TEACHER

Deep Singles

_____ Accuracy _____

_____ Height _____

_____ Power _____

_____ TOTAL EFFICIENCY _____

Short Doubles

_____ Accuracy _____

_____ Height _____

_____ TOTAL EFFICIENCY _____

OVERHEAD FOREHAND

Clear

_____ Accuracy _____

_____ Height _____

_____ Power _____

Drop

_____ Accuracy _____

_____ Height _____

_____ Power _____

Smash

_____ Accuracy _____

_____ Height _____

_____ Power _____

_____ TOTAL EFFICIENCY _____

Class _____

Student _____

Teacher _____

Date _____

STUDENT		TEACHER

OVERHEAD BACKHAND

Clear

	Accuracy	
	Height	
	Power	

Drop

	Accuracy	
	Height	
	Power	

_____ TOTAL EFFICIENCY_____

UNDERHAND

NET CLEARS

Forehand

	Accuracy	
	Height	
	Power	

Backhand

	Accuracy	
	Height	
	Power	

NET DROPS

Forehand

	Accuracy	
	Height	
	Power	

Backhand

	Accuracy	
	Height	
	Power	

_____ TOTAL EFFICIENCY_____

Class _____

Student _____

Teacher _____

Date _____

STUDENT		TEACHER

INTERMEDIATE SHOTS

DRIVES

Forehand

_____	Accuracy	_____
_____	Height	_____
_____	Power	_____

Backhand

_____	Accuracy	_____
_____	Height	_____
_____	Power	_____

Cross Court

_____	Accuracy	_____
_____	Height	_____
_____	Power	_____

_____ TOTAL EFFICIENCY_____

ROUND THE HEAD SHOTS

Clear

_____	Accuracy	_____
_____	Height	_____
_____	Power	_____

Drop

_____	Accuracy	_____
_____	Height	_____
_____	Power	_____

Smash

_____	Accuracy	_____
_____	Height	_____
_____	Power	_____

_____ TOTAL EFFICIENCY_____

Class _____

Student _____

Teacher _____

Date _____

STUDENT   TEACHER

SERVICE RETURNS

SINGLES RETURNS

Straight Clear

	Accuracy	
	Height	
	Power	

Drop

	Accuracy	
	Height	
	Power	

Smash

	Accuracy	
	Height	
	Power	

———————————— TOTAL EFFICIENCY————————————

DOUBLES RETURNS

Straight Drop

	Accuracy	
	Height	
	Power	

Straight One-Half Court

	Accuracy	
	Height	
	Power	

Straight Push

	Accuracy	
	Height	
	Power	

———————————— TOTAL EFFICIENCY————————————

Class _____

Student _____

Teacher _____

Date _____

STUDENT   TEACHER

SMASH RETURNS

Straight Ahead Block

_____ Accuracy _____

_____ Height _____

_____ Power _____

Cross Court Block

_____ Accuracy _____

_____ Height _____

_____ Power _____

Straight Drive

_____ Accuracy _____

_____ Height _____

_____ Power _____

_____ TOTAL EFFICIENCY _____

ADVANCED SHOTS

ADVANCED SERVES

Drive Serve

_____ Accuracy _____

_____ Height _____

_____ Speed _____

_____ TOTAL EFFICIENCY _____

Flick Serve

_____ Accuracy _____

_____ Height _____

_____ Speed _____

_____ TOTAL EFFICIENCY _____

Class _____

Student _____

Teacher _____

Date _____

STUDENT   TEACHER

Backhand Low Service

_____ Accuracy _____

_____ Height _____

_____ TOTAL EFFICIENCY_____

Backhand Smash

_____ Accuracy _____

_____ Height _____

_____ Power _____

_____ TOTAL EFFICIENCY_____

Attacking Clear

_____ Accuracy _____

_____ Height _____

_____ Speed _____

_____ TOTAL EFFICIENCY_____

DROPS

Fast Drop

_____ Accuracy _____

_____ Height _____

_____ Speed _____

Cut Drop

_____ Accuracy _____

_____ Height _____

_____ Speed _____

_____ Deception _____

_____ TOTAL EFFICIENCY_____

Class _____

Student _____

Teacher _____

Date _____

STUDENT   TEACHER

Half Smash

_____ Accuracy   _____

_____ Height   _____

_____ Speed   _____

_____ TOTAL EFFICIENCY_____

Brush Return of Net Shot

_____ Accuracy   _____

_____ Speed   _____

_____ Deception   _____

_____ TOTAL EFFICIENCY_____

Class _____

Student _____

Teacher _____

Date _____